Making a Difference:

Cuff's Guide for
MUNICIPAL
LEADERS

Volume Two

The case for effective governance

GEORGE B. CUFF

brought to you by the publishers of

Municipal World
CANADA'S MUNICIPAL MAGAZINE

Library and Archives Canada Cataloguing in Publication

Cuff, George B.
Making a difference : Cuff's guide for municipal leaders : [the case for effective governance] / George B. Cuff.

ISBN 0-919779-62-X (v.1 : pbk.)
ISBN 978-0-919779-82-2 (v. 2)

1. Municipal government – Canada. 2. City council members – Canada.

I. Title. II. Title: Cuff's guide for municipal leaders. III. Title: Guide for municipal leaders.

JS1715.C83 2002   320.8'5'0971   C2002-904962-8
JS1715*

Published in Canada by
Municipal World Inc.
Box 399, Station Main
St. Thomas, Ontario N5P 3V3
(Union, Ontario N0L 2L0)
2007
mwadmin@municipalworld.com
www.municipalworld.com

ITEM 0059-2
Municipal World — Reg. T.M. in Canada, Municipal World Inc.

Printed on

ENVIRO˙100
PRINT

100%   FSC

CONTENTS

PREFACE

Any task as challenging as authoring a book on local government does not become reality without the assistance of others and the support of one's family. In that regard, I am indebted to my wife Arliss for her support (and patience) of my teaching and consulting endeavours throughout the years and her encouragement to share whatever ideas I might glean from my consulting engagements and experience as a mayor with others in the field. I also appreciate the wisdom and counsel of so many people throughout my career, some of whom have since retired from active roles in local government, and others who continue to labour on. My many clients throughout the years have – perhaps unwittingly – provided many of the ideas for this book (and its predecessor, *Cuff's Guide for Municipal Leaders: a survival guide for elected officials*). So, I gratefully acknowledge their contributions.

Several people have reviewed this text and made many useful suggestions that have improved the clarity of what I have been trying to say. Doug Plamping, Bert Einsiedel and Ron Born have all acted as reviewers and their thoughts and suggestions have been appreciated. Doug and Ron have both been chief administrative officers, as well as associates of mine. Bert retired from a very successful life as a university professor and taught with my wife and me during a seminar in Jakarta, Indonesia. All are cherished friends.

I have been blessed by God throughout my career in having an avocation (local politics) and a vocation that have met, providing me with a very interesting life. The ideas that I share in this book are a part of that experience.

I admire all who have chosen to serve their fellow residents with integrity in any capacity, but particularly those in political life. My desire is to make that road somewhat less problematic by contributing to a better understanding of what is expected of those who lead our communities.

Chapter 1

GOVERNANCE: THE NEED TO GET IT RIGHT

Most councils and local boards do not possess either the right tools or approaches to govern and manage their businesses appropriately during the term of office and to finish with a real sense of accomplishment.

This is perhaps the most troubling observation I might make after a career working with such organizations. (I refer to both councils and boards here with reference to the governing body throughout the text, though I refer to councils as the primary audience.) Those elected (or appointed) to the governing body often lack a sound, fundamental understanding of their task and how it could be accomplished most effectively.

Communities and the organizations established to deliver services to their residents are best served when those who lead are clear in their priorities, objectives, tasks and focused in their resolve. Citizens expect those at the helm to steer in a prudent manner, making the best use of the resources designated for justifiable priorities. They trust that those whom they have elected will ensure that the necessary services are being provided in an effective, cost-efficient manner. They rely on the assumption that the rule of law will be adhered to by those who act in leadership, as well as service capacities. Most citizens would see these expectations as reasonable.

With some hesitancy and regret, but based on extensive experience over three decades, I note that municipalities (and other similar public sector bodies) across Canada are often poorly served by their elected leaders. This assessment does not stem from any concern about possessing the right motivation. Rather, the underlying failure relates to an absence of understanding of the meaning of effective governance and, in light of that, what changes should be made to the present model in order to make it more functional. Often, council members sense that what they are doing is adding little value to the well-being of their communities, but they are unsure of how to make the changes or adjustments that would result in stronger, more focused leadership. Some council members are so delighted to have been elected that they lack any sense of "is that all there is?" Many others, though, are plagued by an inner voice that prods them into asking more penetrating questions about the significance of their role.

My Purpose

This is a rather strong opening statement and pretext for a book devoted to "getting it right." While I may not adequately resolve or even fully identify all the core issues, the primary purpose of this text is to help municipal councils (and any other governing bodies to which these same principles apply) add value to their respective communities (and organizations) through the understanding and application of the principles and techniques of effective governance.

I have frequently heard the following comments:

> What is it that I am doing here? This is not the type of service that I had in mind.

> I really question the value that I add to this organization!

> If that's the role of the administration, what are we council members supposed to be doing?

Unfortunately, and all too frequently, comments such as these are expressed by those elected or appointed to senior positions within public sector organizations. People are very concerned about their ability and potential to make a difference in organizations where they are called or chosen to serve. These frustrations are not the result of inadequate skills or a lack of desire to serve. Rather, and far more frequently, they arise out of an inadequate orientation to the task and a lack of training on the essence of their roles. Thus, there is misunderstanding as to what is really expected.

A Caveat

It is not my intention to provide an exhaustive account of all aspects that affect and relate to governance. Those described in this book are significant, but not all-inclusive. It needs to be clear that any legislation pertaining to local government in a given jurisdiction must be followed by any council wishing to change its model, or wishing to add to or subtract from certain of its powers.

Repeating the Past

There are many reasons why people run for elected office. One of the more common reasons is the sense of being able to do better than the incumbents. While this may seem, at first blush, to be immodest, without a heightened personal sense of being a capable and caring person, it is unlikely that a political neophyte will have the drive and enthusiasm to be successful. There are a number of first-rate elected officials serving their communities because they rightly felt that their predecessors had either grown old and disinterested in their avocation, or had long since lost the fervour to make things better.

The notion of challenging the status quo is essential if positive change is to occur. If council members do not question the current pattern of doing the business of the municipality, it is very likely that not much will change in their term of office. History will, in fact, repeat itself. In some respects, that may not be all bad. There will always be some policies of prior terms that are quite acceptable, and in which no change is necessary. Where these are effective and attuned to the current circumstances, change may not be required or even desired.

Changes to the current system of governance must be considered at the outset of any term of office. In the absence of a clear and effective set of principles to guide the role of elected officials, the chosen patterns of behaviour are more likely to reflect the style of those previously holding governance positions. New people are elected and the work begins. Sometimes, there are very urgent issues that require the attention of council; little time may be set aside for any training. The administration (and/or the public) wants answers to outstanding questions. Meetings of council are scheduled and conducted according to the established rules of the day, and the flow of business looks very much like it did during the previous term of office, with the exception of some new faces in old chairs. In effect, nothing changes because the system has become unresponsive to change.

For some new members, governance is perceived as an extension of their previous roles on a local service club or a provincial organization, or as an extension of the type of day-to-day work that a newly elected member has been involved in throughout their career. The main task for most is becoming elected. The notion that this was only the beginning step on a much longer journey may be foreign to them. And, while it may be possible for new members of council to be of some value to their respective communities, the needs of their citizens will not be met unless they understand the expected and appropriate roles of a local elected official.

Governance is a New Concept

It is not unusual that a council struggles with its role early in its term. Governance, for most people, is new. It is not an extension of what they have done before, nor can it be likened to other areas of service. Governance is different in that:

➤ it is limited in a municipality to the elected body of council members;

➤ it does not simply stem from other skills used in other walks of life;

➤ it is distinct from the work of the administration;

➤ other than the legislation, there is no real job description for elected officials; and

➤ those elected to govern may understand the concept quite differently and act in very different ways.

Communities are not well served by elected officials and appointed staff members striving to duplicate the efforts of one another. The reason for establishing two distinct roles ought to be clear: we need both if our communities are to function as well as intended. If the issue is one of needing more staff to carry out the day-to-day work, the solution is not going to be found in electing more members of council. Similarly, if the citizens complain about being under-represented, the solution will not lie in hiring additional cashiers or maintenance staff.

What Does Governance Require?

Governance requires the following:

➤ an appreciation of people;

➤ a desire to serve others;

➤ a willingness to learn;

➤ a willingness to listen to one's colleagues;

➤ a readiness to compromise on issues;

➤ an understanding of the issues;

➤ research, reading and checking out the facts;

➤ an understanding of the decision-making process;

➤ an understanding of everyone's roles, including their own; and

➤ patience.

Governance is unique. It requires a particular skill set and an abundance of patience, as well as a willingness to be of service to others – even when it might appear that those being served are not particularly appreciative of the service, or the servers.

The Bottom Line

It my hope that this text will assist in examining why governance at the local level has proven to be so difficult; how a lack of role definition contributes to this dilemma; what defines quality governance; the tools and powers of governance; and the building blocks for a new style of effective governance.

Chapter 2
LEADERSHIP TOOLS AND PROCESSES

The public expects its leaders to lead. Every community has issues that need to be addressed and decisions that need to be made. Leaders are expected to be capable of making informed choices, and bringing their sense of the public will to bear on the issues.

This is not a task for the faint of heart, nor for those who would be dictators. Rather, the public expects those whom it elects to understand the issues confronting their community; to discern the strengths and weaknesses of viable alternatives and choices; and to make those decisions necessary and essential to good government.

Quality first-class leadership requires those leading to possess the basic tools for making clear decisions on issues that require the governing body to get involved. That is, leaders must understand what their role implies – and what it does not. They must, therefore, have a clear picture of that which distinguishes elected officials from administrators, policy from procedure, and leadership from management.

What Are the Basic Tools?

Good decision making does not just happen. It is a reflection of the effective utilization of the tools of decision making applied using a maximum degree of common sense and a minimum of personal ego. These tools include the following.

Integrity – The most important tool of good decision making lies within the make-up of each council member. While not everyone will have the same academic background or base of related experience, each can and should possess high personal ethics that are reflected in how they make decisions, and how they consider the well-being of others.

Respect for the input of others – Good decision making is never intended to be a one-person show. A council is a composite of a number of points of view and experiences. Its members seldom think the same on significant issues. While a council may readily be drawn towards the same solution, the initial discussion gives weight to the notion that others do indeed think differently.

Members of an effective council listen to each other's opinions, even when it may be clear that the opinions are widely divergent. While the positions being taken may be poles apart, there is often a kernel of truth in the advice and input of others that may radically affect the decision.

Respect is shown both verbally and non-verbally. The former is reflected in an encouraging comment to the other members of council. The latter is reflected in body language (leaning in vs. leaning away; nodding one's head in agreement vs. rolling one's eyes as if to say "Did you just say what I thought you did?!").

Respect for the advice and expertise of the administration – One of the keys to good decision making lies in the relationship that develops between members of council and the senior administration. Where there is strong support for the administration and the effort that they put forward in ensuring council has access to quality information and advice, one finds an openness of shared information and a respect for alternative views. Council members need to appreciate that the administration, while not necessarily parallel to council in its thinking, is at least adding an opinion that is well-founded and thoughtful. Such opinions are based on the expertise gained by the administration collectively, often over many years. These opinions are refined in discussions with their counterparts from other jurisdictions, and through a review of the literature.

Thoughtful process – Quality decision making is a reflection of an ongoing process that involves a number of people, and a wealth of varying ideas. While some decisions seem to be made on the basis of very little thought, that is often due to the fact that they are either a repeat of prior decisions, or are based on solid policies that have stood the test of time. Many other decisions, however, result only after the governing body has thought through the issues and considered the consequences, as well as the possible impacts on other policies. Governing bodies (such as a municipal council) that are charged with issues of importance need people who are prepared to reflect, rather than simply rush into what later turns out to be a hasty and ill-considered decision.

Reflection on the alternatives – A community wants to elect those who understand that every big decision has within its scope a number of potential alternatives. Residents expect that, as leaders, council members will consider those alternatives and determine the strengths and weaknesses of each argument.

Democracy on the local level is important to people. They like the notion that they are being served by their fellow citizens, rather than somebody in a remote community who may not care about their issues. They may not always agree with the choices a council makes, but they respect the fact that others in their community have been charged with the responsibility of deciding on matters that are important to the community.

WHAT LEADERS DO ...

☑   Focus on the Right Things

☑   See the Larger Landscape

☑   Focus on Choices, Not Tasks

☑   Understand Relative Importance

Leaders Focus on the Right Things

Elected officials seldom add value by:

▶   pouring over the minute details of a budget spreadsheet;

▶   memorizing the procedural by-law;

▶   requiring the administration to bring forward for approval their procedures for implementing council's decisions;

▶   resurrecting old issues (i.e. those discussed by previous councils and determined not to be in the public interest);

▶   focusing on what tasks their management will tackle next;

▶   regularly attending or chairing meetings of management;

▶   reviewing the personnel file of anyone other than the chief administrative officer;

▶   questioning the choice of one supplier over another, when both sell essentially the same products;

▶   visiting job sites and speaking with the employees of the municipality or contracted companies; or

► explaining the difference between goals and objectives in a corporate planning or strategy session.

Case in Point

In one Nova Scotia municipality, a member of council advised that he was well within his rights to demand a detailed accounting of the full budget for that city. He, along with his colleagues, poured over every line item in a substantial budget, requesting explanations of why certain codes were required, why one item could not be coded to a different account, why the costs went up by more than the cost of living, what rationale there might be for a difference in the salaries of two relatively senior personnel, whether or not a local supplier might be considered, and so on.

At the end of the day, and after initially criticizing the administration for bringing in a budget that was well beyond where this council wanted to position its mill rates, the budget was actually increased by a percentage point.

The foregoing process did not, of course, address the new council's priorities or what services were being delivered that could be re-considered. Instead, the focus (and thus the devil) was on the details. The larger picture (and any real sense of council exercising its leadership as a newly elected body) was lost entirely.

Leaders See the Larger Landscape

So, what is wrong with a detailed examination of the budget? After all, a member of council can learn a lot about the municipal business by being fully briefed as to where the funds are being spent. Further, requesting a detailed accounting will ensure that the administration is clear that council is really "in charge" and that no stone will be left unturned in its pursuit of cost efficiencies. While that may be true, a council that insists on being briefed on the details of each issue may run the much more costly risk of being unaware as to the story being told by the larger picture. In truth, the details won't matter if the big-picture policy choices are not kept front and centre.

It may be that affording the council with the option of receiving a much more detailed presentation of the budget by the appropriate officials during a day set aside for that purpose will be of some benefit. Members of council may gain a better appreciation of the scope of the budget and the services being offered by the municipality. Service options might be discussed in this briefing session, and alternative approaches debated. Where such a debate is deemed to benefit all of council, then such matters could be moved onto a more formal agenda. But, simply pouring over the detailed budget without the larger perspective will be

akin to drinking from a fire hose when a glass of water would have suf-
ficed. Council members, in order to be effective, have to take a
broadly-based strategic perspective of the issues – not one that has as
its focus the details of an operation.

Case in Point

*I can recall being asked to review a department of a British Columbia city.
Foolishly, I accepted the assignment early in my career as a management
consultant. It was the last time I agreed to review a single department. The
fact of the matter is that no civic department can truly be assessed without
reference to the other departments. Is the task simply to review whether or
not the department is doing its tasks well, or is the more important task to
determine whether or not the mandate of that department is appropriate
given the scope and mandate of the other sister departments? What if some
of the department's tasks could be performed better by others in the organization? What if the tasks need not be done at all, based on a change in
direction by the organization as a whole?*

*If reference to the big picture is missing, improving the details is unlikely to
be of much value.*

Leaders Focus on Choices, Not Tasks

Elected officials are elected to choose what to do – as opposed to how
to do it efficiently. Thus, for example, the public receives value from its
council when it makes a decision as to the priority of key projects, not
when council insists on its own inspection or detailed examination of
the credentials of each competing bid. The first decision places the emphasis on the *role* of a council and the absolute importance of every
council determining the priority to be accorded to critical issues. Examining the credentials of various bidders is hardly the work of an elected
body. If a council finds it difficult to allocate such a task to its senior
officials, then there is a much larger issue that needs to be tackled – i.e.
whether or not the council has sufficient confidence in the work or
judgment of its officials.

It is not that "how to do things" is unimportant. It's just not the job of
elected officials to be in that business. Unfortunately, local governments have spent far too much time indulging the interests of their
elected officials in how things get done, rather than re-directing the focus of a council on their own mandate of governing. This historic approach to the real essence of governance has been wrong-headed and
has relegated the impact of those governing to those matters that appear
on the surface to be interesting, but that are sadly those pertaining to

the less relevant and important. Bureaucracies, large and small, have allowed, encouraged or welcomed the intrusion of elected officials into their realm. The effect is to negate the potential of effective leadership on issues of importance to the community, and to allow the bureaucracies to avoid their own responsibilities.

Leaders Understand Relative Importance

What is more important:

► Casting the vision, or passing the accounts payable?

► Determining the preferred direction of new growth, or questioning the planner's credentials?

► Meeting with community leaders to discuss a new downtown strategy, or identifying problems with parking enforcement?

► Identifying a new policy direction, or helping the administration draft a new procedure to support an existing policy of questionable validity?

► Discussing how the community can become the focal point for cultural or athletic events in the region, or sitting through meetings of organizations whose business has a limited to negligible impact on the council's agenda?

► Discussing the official community plan in often heated community meetings where disagreements arise because of differing aspirations for the community, or accepting the latest plan amendment to a plan that has long since become stale-dated/redundant?

Leadership requires people of vision, and the courage to state that vision with clarity. Leaders speak to priorities more than process; to results more than plans; to public expectations more than questionnaires; and to next year more than last week.

Chapter 3

GOVERNANCE IS NOT ...

The key to becoming an effective governing body is coming to an understanding of what governance is, and what it is not. Our principal failure in local governments across Canada is not developing a clear picture of what the governing body is to do. Much of this has obviously been passed down through generations, where those governing were viewed largely as an extension of those administering. The need to articulate the differences was not apparent, and the system of government in municipalities was cobbled together so that it "worked." The administration was expected to handle the day-to-day matters that appeared to be straightforward, while those matters that seemed a bit different or were obviously significant were taken to council for a decision. The lines of demarcation between the two were muddy at best (and in many instances have remained so).

We have marginalized the real value of governance in municipalities by associating it or making it synonymous with the day-to-day challenges of administration. In doing so, we have reduced the importance of both, and have made it very difficult for managers to be seen as professionals and for political leaders to be seen as laypeople. I have often wondered why people who serve on elected councils as well as on health or school boards have expressed real concern about the increasing salaries for municipal managers, while approving significantly higher compensation for those toiling in the other professions. Could it be that council members believe that anyone can do the job of a chief administrative officer (or a department head), but that management positions in the health and education fields require professionals with specialized training? (As the body of knowledge and the profession of local government matures, I would expect to see more rigorous standards, higher qualifications and presumably enhanced salaries evolve.)

We have committed a grave injustice to those who are legitimately managing in the field of local government. This is a profession that requires people who are skilled in managing a wide range of tasks, many of which require quite different capabilities. A chief administrative officer must possess an understanding of local government finance, a variety of pieces of legislation, politics, community services, transportation, engineering, protective services, libraries, sports facilities, social services and an array of other services that may be particular to that jurisdiction (eg. agriculture, assessment, airports, marinas, museums, seniors homes, and so on).

Results of Blending

In blending the responsibilities of elected and appointed officials, we have reduced managers to administrative assistants and clerks, capable of carrying out orders (perhaps), but incapable of providing sound leadership and careful judgment to the discharge of responsible managerial functions and the implementation of council policies. We have also detracted from the skills required by those elected to govern by aligning these with managerial tasks, and not identifying their true distinctiveness.

Case in Point

We have seen a number of municipalities where the title of the senior administrator is "clerk" or "clerk-administrator" (or treasurer). In the vast majority of these cases, particularly in Ontario, Nova Scotia and British Columbia, the position tends to become viewed as that of a clerk or assistant to council. While there may be some historical value in retaining titles, those that govern (and manage) must not forget that the position will be viewed by themselves and others on the modern understanding of the title. In some instances, the "clerk" has devolved into the keeper of minutes and the printer of agendas, with all instructions being given directly by council to department heads.

An additional danger in this is that the vacuum in leadership created will be filled by either the strongest department head, or by the elected officials. Either result could be disastrous for the organization.

If your organization retains a title that does not accurately describe the role of the position as chief administrative officer, ensure that other mechanisms are in place so that the role of the position does not devolve.

It is little wonder that the municipal field has struggled in terms of developing, retaining or attracting a suitable talent pool of capable senior managers who could adequately manage any of our big cities. We simply have not made the position very attractive, in large measure because we have been unable to identify just what a manager does in relation to the role of council. Becoming a senior executive of either a provincial or federal department or health authority in Canada is often more financially attractive – and definitely more stable. For the most part, those elected to political posts in the other two orders of government understand with greater clarity their roles and recognize those as being distinct from that of the administrators. There is a healthier sense of separation than one finds in local government. And yet, in many instances, the role of a CAO (the chief administrative officer is the title most frequently used in the local government context, and the one we will utilize in this text) is of greater challenge due to its scope. Further, a CAO is considerably more prone to public comment due to the intense public and media scrutiny placed on senior public officials in the municipal arena compared to that of other senior public sector posts.

The issue is not: Have we properly identified the role of a senior municipal administrator? No, the more essential question is: Do we really know what we expect of our elected officials, and is their role sufficiently distinct? Without this clarity, how will it be possible to improve the governance mandate? How will we address the growing degree of conflict between elected and appointed officials if we remain unable to ascertain with some degree of assurance that we know what it is they are to do?

Being an Elected Official is Not ...

Citizens, often with no experience in municipal administration, are elected by their fellow citizens *to govern*. They are not elected to *manage*. Whenever council members are involved in the latter, they are operating outside of their role. Perhaps a sports analogy would help. General managers in the world of hockey pursue and sign certain players to fulfill the team's need for a goaltender. One could search high and low for a goaltender who could also fill the role of a centreman or right winger, and come up empty-handed. Why? Because that is not what a goaltender is asked or expected to be. And yet, the goaltender is "on the team" and fulfilling a very important role. The positions on a hockey team are not interchangeable. Nor are the roles in the world of governance and being an elected official.

Becoming an elected official is not an invitation to become an understudy of a department head or CAO. Nor is it based on the need for more administrative staff. Nor is it an invitation to oversee all of the functions of each administrator so as to determine what faults have been allowed to go unpunished by a previous council. While elected officials in Canada's smallest communities may be called on to also umpire ball games on the weekend, or participate in a "clean-up campaign," these tasks are apart from the role of an elected official. One is never elected to become an administrator. And, regardless of the person's own business background (or even prior experience as a civil servant), the process of becoming elected ensures that those who wish to govern are separated from the tasks of day-to-day management.

I defined "governance" in Volume One (*Cuff's Guide for Municipal Leaders: a survival guide for elected officials*) as:

> ... the process of exercising corporate leadership by the policy-making authority (i.e. council) on behalf of the public to the organization as a whole, in terms of its purpose, control and future and overseeing the organization to ensure that its mandate is achieved.

Thus, this process requires:

► the exercise of leadership (i.e. making policy choices);

► direct involvement by the council as the policy leaders;

► an understanding of public preferences and wants;

► leadership to the whole organization in terms of how it delivers services;

► a clear understanding of the preferred future of the community so that the organization is structured to deliver services that are applicable; and

► the establishment of control measures that ensure that the leaders can maintain an awareness of whether or not the aims of the organization (i.e. the goals and priorities of the council) are being achieved.

If governance is a compilation of what we have just described, then it cannot, at the same time, include the following:

► management of departments;

► review of individual accounts;

► the approval of accounting procedures;

► supervision of individual employees other than the CAO;

► development of procedures and regulations;

► review of detailed bidding procedures to ensure that the "right" people were awarded the tender;

► involvement in the hiring of anyone (other than the CAO);

➤ approval of individual wage adjustments (other than the CAO); or

➤ review and approval of performance assessments (other than the CAO).

Steering vs. Rowing

In a nutshell, the act of governing is, and must be, distinctly different than that of administration. Some have used the illustration of steering and rowing a boat. The guidance to the boat is provided by the captain who understands the destination and the best way of getting there safely. The captain sets the course and makes any needed mid-course adjustments. The crew ensures that the rowing occurs. In other words, they conduct those activities needed to achieve the direction or course set out by the captain. If everyone steers, the desired course will be muddled, and no movement will be made in terms of getting there. If everyone rows, the result will be akin to the fellow who exclaimed, "I may be lost, but I'm making record time!" Results are best achieved when everyone understands their role, and when they steadfastly refuse to take on the roles assigned to others.

Case in Point

A rural municipality in north central Alberta called to ask for my assistance in conducting a review of their organization. They'd had a number of staff turn-overs recently and considerable difficulties balancing the role of councillor with that of administrator. I called to set a date for my first round of interviews, only to be told that no one on council was available, as all were engaged in interviewing for the position of Superintendent of Works.

When I did begin the interviews, I inquired as to why everyone was tied up. Of course, I was informed that interviews were taking place over a couple of days. When I asked what happened to the last fellow, the response was predictable: he had been fired. Not suitable, so they said. I asked whether or not the same approach had been used, and the answer was "yes." Every member of council, as well as the CAO, was afforded the opportunity to review and score the resumes, and those getting the top marks were invited in for the interview. The fact that the preferred choice of the CAO never made the shortlist was not considered given the reliance on democracy.

The interviews were held; a vote was taken; an offer made; the candidate was hired; and before he could buy a house and move his family in, he was fired. (No one thought to ask: how did we make another major mistake?) When I asked who was responsible for the poor decision making, the answer was ... "I guess we all are."

Who should have been involved? Certainly not the members of council. They were not elected to take on the job of the CAO. They were not elected

to enable the CAO to avoid the heat of close scrutiny. They were not elected because of their vast repertoire of recruitment skills and experience at senior levels of municipalities. (Even the experts in that business get it wrong every so often, and they have been practising their craft for years!)

Effective governing bodies realize what their roles are and stick to them. Becoming the personnel department, or replacing the CAO, are not included on that list.

Governance is Not Advocating for External ABCs

Some mistake a council's governance role with that of advocating for various ABCs (agencies, boards and committees) within the community. While volunteering and helping local groups with their projects and causes is generally to be supported, and while members of council often find their beginnings as members of a local group, the role of a council member vis-a-vis local groups changes after becoming elected. No longer can, or should, a member of council presume that their role allows them to advocate for this or that group. A member of council needs to place the interests and objectives of council first and foremost in terms of priorities (outside of family and work). At times, that may bring the member of council to a place where they can no longer support the objectives or timing of a particular local group. It is not that the local group has suddenly become one of the antagonists of the council. Rather, the onus is on the member of council to act in their primary role as a member of council, rather than in the roles held prior to being elected to council.

Quite simply, the advocates for any agency, board or committee are its chair and full members. Anyone other than a member of council could serve as the primary spokesperson and/or advocate. No member of council should allow their name to be nominated as an executive of any group other than council, unless that group is a regional, provincial or national body that is comprised of other elected officials representing other local jurisdictions.

The Biblical adage, "You cannot serve God and manna" comes to mind. You need to make a choice: either serve the interests of the full community, or choose to step down and serve the mandate and objectives of an interest group.

Keys to Governance

In summary, governance is not:

► managing the administration or a department thereof;

- ► focusing on the details;
- ► identifying with specific groups in the community;
- ► advocating for special interest groups;
- ► passing the policies and carrying them out;
- ► developing procedures, job descriptions, tender documents, etc.;
- ► hiring staff below the CAO; or
- ► appraising staff below the CAO.

The key to achieving the right balance lies, in part, with helping elected officials understand that their roles are indeed quite different. Secondly, it must be clearly explained what those roles entail. It is one thing to simply declare that there are distinctions, and quite another to define what they are.

Therein lies one of the fundamental flaws of local governance. While we have placed considerable emphasis on declaring the roles of elected and appointed officials to be different (i.e. "you set the policies and I administer them"), we have spent precious little time and resources describing such roles.

Chapter 4

WHY COUNCIL GOVERNANCE?

As someone who has assessed local governments and their practices across Canada, and as someone who has taught local government administration, it is evident that most of those serving as managers in our municipalities are competent and experienced professionals. Most are quite capable of discharging the day-to-day tasks to which they have been assigned. They do not need anyone other than their own supervisor to provide counsel and assistance, and most resent the inference that they do.

If the foregoing is largely true, and I would suggest that it is, then just why do we need an elected body of laypeople to act as governors of the system?

Acting on Our Behalf

The western world is based on a system of democracy in which we elect our leaders. As members of the public, we place our expectation of quality and informed public choices, through an election process, in the governing body that is expected to make wise policy decisions on our behalf. Given the limitations of such a system, we ensure its success by surrounding our elected leaders with those who have been trained in appropriate disciplines, and who are able to implement the decisions of the policy-making authority. This separation is designed so as to ensure that the question of "what is to be done?" is made by the elected body; the question of "how will it be done?" is delegated to those trained and experienced in handling such issues. In theory, at least, that is a capsule account of the distinctions.

So, while it should be apparent that the administration is quite capable of making the management decisions facing the municipality, the elected official stands at the centre of any democracy. Members of the elected body are held to account for all policy decisions, including how much financial support the municipality requires to run its operations; what programs and services are to be provided; to what degree such services are supported (or subsidized) by the public purse; what type of development is to be pursued; and other similar issues.

It is also important to recognize that elected officials are held to account for the behaviour and decisions of their administration. Thus, while council members should delegate administrative matters to those trained in such issues, accountability for results rests inevitably with those elected to office. They cannot simply pass poor decisions off to the hired staff, but must stand behind their actions. Such recognition does not, however, justify the day-to-day involvement by council members (either individually or collectively) in matters that have been delegated or legislated as being the purview of the administration.

What is the Objective? Reflecting the Public Will

Governance is about understanding and then reflecting the public will in council's decisions. While there are times when a council leads based on what it feels are decisions in the best interests of the community, regardless of what a vote of its residents might indicate, in most circumstances the presumed "public will" prevails.

If it grasps with clarity what the will of the public is or would be in their community, council should be able to lead with confidence that it has made the right decisions. This is an elusive and ill-defined objective for most, given that it relies on the sense that council members consistently comprehend what fellow residents would choose if they were confronted by the same issues or questions and with access to the same information as council.

Other than the public input that is required by provincial legislation (eg. planning matters), every council functions based on the hope (or sense) that its view of the issues will reflect the view that a majority of fellow citizens would hold if they were similarly briefed. Given the practical impossibility of seeking the will of the public on a frequent basis through some polling technique, a council is faced with the implied requirement to seek the will of its residents on matters deemed critical or of significance to the community.

What Defines a "Significant Issue"?

Council needs to identify those issues that are of sufficient significance to warrant the search for informed public input. In very large communities, there may be few city-wide issues that would qualify as such. The need to annex neighbouring communities might be one example. Dramatic changes to the current transportation system might also qualify. In a small community, engaging neighbouring communities in a multi-use recreation complex would likely qualify as "significant." Authorizing a major airport on the boundaries, or changing the location of the downtown core would also seem to most citizens as altering the nature of their community. Quite simply, the identification of such issues is unique to each community and may only occur on a very infrequent basis. The magnitude and complexity of a policy issue often determines its significance. Whether or not it is controversial depends more on the nature and organization of competing interests involved in the issue.

Case in Point

A municipality in the southern Okanagan area of British Columbia called to ask for assistance in conducting a review of their organization. In the course of the review, we discussed the advantages of having the community involved in helping council identify the key issues facing the town. Council agreed to have me facilitate a community issues forum, and plans were put in place to advertise the event.

When I asked as to expected turnout, the council indicated that likely 30-50 people would attend. What they had not thought of was that their previous council meeting had featured a presentation from a prospective developer who wanted to build multi-family developments along the lake front. The day of the event arrived and the crowds came; in fact, they kept coming. Instead of 30-50, we had over 300 folks in attendance! And, while their primary motive was obviously on preserving the waterfront as it was, the audience participated generously in identifying the values of their town, the community's identity, key community priorities and future goals.

For this community, the thought that their council might alter a significant portion of what the residents held to be inviolate was enough to prompt them into action. Not all community planning sessions are as well-attended on a per capita basis, but then few have the "good fortune" of being planned on the heels of a controversial event.

Need for Balance

The beauty of a council is that it is made up of people whose views are disparate. That is, in the absence of a party system in most local governments across Canada (and that's a good thing), council members tend to think independently and incongruently. While they may cloister together on a common policy or direction, each member comes at an issue with a fresh set of eyes, and often little to gain or lose. This affords council the time and inclination to weigh the issues and seek balance in their disposition.

Community groups do not do that – nor do they pretend to. In most instances, they have clear positions on their favourite issues, and are quite keen to have members of council hear their wisdom on the topic.

Seldom do they argue that council ought to look more carefully at the alternatives to their advice! Rather, they would have council believe that there are no suitable alternatives.

In most instances, the public feels that it has chosen a body of citizens who are elected to represent their views on matters of importance to their community. Continually seeking affirmation on direction may have the effect of diminishing public confidence, rather than enhancing it. (Having said this, I am aware that there is no such thing as too much consultation in some communities!) Each council needs to be aware of what sensitivities their community would have to what types of issues, and act accordingly – whether required by legislation to do so, or not.

Why council governance? Because we rely on a group of men and women to think issues through carefully, weigh the potential good or harm to the fabric of the community, and make decisions that any group of like-minded citizens would view as sustainable.

Chapter 5

CLARITY OF ROLE DISTINCTIONS — THE GENESIS OF PROBLEMS

Why does this issue of "governance" tend to be so widely misunderstood and undervalued? In my opinion, and based on discussions with countless others involved in local governments across Canada, our failure to stake out the ground clearly at the outset has paved the way for misunderstanding and role confusion that forms a part of the culture in most of our communities.

We have allowed the most significant aspect of what a council does to be replaced by the confused yet prevalent notion that a council's role is not really that different from that of the administration. This lack of understanding can be traced to several sources, discussed below.

No Single Agency Across Canada Sees Education of Members of Governing Bodies As Its Role

We have seen the rise of various publicly-funded academic institutions and schools across Canada, which have attempted to give high priority to the training of municipal officials. While this effort is laudable, and may have had a positive impact over the years, there has not been any successful attempt to structure a program for elected officials that would be recognized Canada-wide, and would suit the varying needs of each province. Most of the programs that do exist are either viewed as "one-offs" or are add-ons to an existing array of programs offered by the same institution. While there are potential players in this regard, no one has yet stepped up to the plate to put in motion a well thought-out Canadian "local governance training institute." Hopefully, this matter will be addressed, perhaps through a consortium of educational institutions, departments of municipal affairs, municipal associations and experienced consultants.

Until such time as a body with cross-Canada credibility (such as the Federation of Canadian Municipalities or a council of municipal deputy ministers) undertakes this initiative, the results will be as they have been – less than satisfactory.

No Consistent Effort to Educate Candidates Prior to Election

The business of being on a council is a serious undertaking indeed. Vast numbers of dollars are being spent annually in developing new municipal infrastructure. Yet, those leading our municipalities are not expected to require any education for their tasks. While one could argue that council members are simply expected to be politicians (i.e. the spokespersons for the public), the fact of the matter is quite different. Council members (indeed all those involved in various aspects of governance) must come to understand how a fairly complex system works – including such interesting and generally new topics as:

► what budgets and financial statements reflect;

► how funds are raised;

► the basis of taxation;

► the concept of user fees;

► policy making;

► business plans;

► role of an auditor;

► legislation and by-laws;

► infrastructure planning, development and rehabilitation; and

► a plethora of other topics.

It is obviously not appropriate to have political leaders thoroughly immersed in such topics; but, it is essential that they understand the basics of how the system of local government functions. Although there has been some attempt to provide pre-election orientation seminars for those contemplating a career in local government (or even serving one term on the local council), this has not been the track record across Canada, nor have the provincial associations and their membership endorsed this concept. Thus, while the media and the public may bring the limited degree of relevant knowledge of elected officials into the spotlight from time to time (often because of some local disaster), the issue soon passes or is limited to the community where a member of council has brought the community into disrepute. It should not take a major event through which the community experiences embarrassment to place the spotlight on the training and business acumen of elected officials.

Quite simply, the business of being on a council is important enough to warrant some training before the role is accepted. Too often, a member of council presumes a degree of understanding immediately after an election that was not obvious the day before. In order to guard against the notion that an election conveys both wisdom and knowledge, a planned program of training for all potential members of local (and regional) governments across Canada is a concept that ought to be nurtured within those organizations that can help to orchestrate such training. This is a complex and difficult profession. Allowing new members to enter a profession wherein the need for relevant training is not required seems to auger against this notion.

Council Members Not Focused on Governance as Part of Orientation

Those communities that routinely provide their new councils with a thorough orientation program often miss the very essence of the task at hand. Elections are an exercise in democracy; they are designed to distinguish those for whom the public expresses the greatest degree of confidence in their capacity to become policy makers.

People do not campaign on their knowledge of local government. The talent pool in that regard would be thin indeed. Most of those elected to positions of leadership in local government have backgrounds that are largely incidental to the mandate of the municipality. They may be from any number of professions and occupations, and some from none at all. With respect and quite simply, it really does not matter.

The reason most people are elected has very little to do with their occupation. They are not being elected to manage some aspect of local government. Rather, the public at least understands that those they elect are expected to provide governance leadership to the municipality in terms of the presumed policy interests and preferences of the public.

Unfortunately, those administering local government often miss the mistake being made, over and over again. They believe that what they do is all that matters to the life of any community; thus, they believe those being elected will need to understand how they "do it." Many administrators do not understand that a governing body has a mandate much different from the one fulfilled by those actually administering the system.

As a result, orientations are built around such misunderstandings. Instead of trying to maximize the newly elected person's view of what their role entails, the focus is intentionally placed on what each department head does, and the essence of the administrative agenda. Tours of the municipality and its infrastructure are planned, and council members may even be given an introduction to the people who really make city hall function – the front line administrative staff.

Most senior administrators appear reluctant to devote special attention to the distinct role of an elected official. Why is this? Several reasons come to mind.

► These people, regardless of how green in their job, are my bosses. How am I supposed to tell them their roles?

► Some of these folks have been around local government a long time. Why not just let them "buddy up" with the new members, and slowly educate them into their new roles?

► My previous councils seemed to enjoy my role so much, I'm not sure what it is that they are supposed to do that is any different. How can we start again and get it right?

► How do I convince the returning head of council (known as mayor in the vast majority of instances across Canada – in other places as lord mayor, chair, reeve or warden) that he or she and council colleagues had their roles wrong during the last term?

Small community administrators may be reluctant to engage in any formalized training on governance due to a fear of being seen to lecture their new bosses on what their roles entail. Sometimes, this reluctance appears to genuinely reflect the opinion that a member of council is expected to become fully acquainted with the work and expertise of the administration. Such people truly believe that the single most important distinction between the two roles lies in the fact that "real" administrators get paid for their work, while members of council receive a pittance in lieu of giving up much of their family time.

In order for the orientation to be effective and more than lip service, administrators need to feel confident placing the emphasis of orientation squarely on council's principal tasks. This may be in spite of the fact that some members of a council believe that God or the process of osmosis equipped them fully for their tasks on election night. (To those individuals, I note that even the Bible places an emphasis on the need for study.)

Chapter 6

WHAT MAKES A GOOD COUNCIL MEMBER?

Fortunately, there is no one academic or experiential background that would define a "good" council member. Otherwise, many of those elected today would be questioning why they or their colleagues ever thought to place their names forward for the public's consideration! Members of council come from all types of backgrounds, ranging from lawyer to legal secretary, interior designer to web designer, machinist to mechanical engineer, breadwinner to breadmaker, firefighter to former police chief, farmer to fisher.

There are, however, a number of criteria that help ensure the success of such ventures into public life.

While there are no set requirements in law relative to what makes a good council member, there are legal considerations in terms of who is permitted to run for municipal office. These are generally consistent across Canada, and essentially require all candidates to be Canadian citizens, be over 18 years of age, be resident in the municipality, not be serving a sentence of imprisonment, etc.

In addition to meeting those entry requirements, there are criteria that will determine whether or not a member of council will be successful as a contributing member of any council.

Willingness to Serve Others

Anyone thinking of running for public office needs to begin at a common point – a very strong desire to serve others. Without that basis, the challenges that will confront every member of council at some point in every term of office might be met with the cry, "Why did I ever allow myself to be talked into running for a position on council?"

Becoming elected is generally not based on the amount of money one is likely to make. The small stipend paid in most communities is often less than one could earn serving as a stockperson in a store or as a server in a local restaurant. While there are *per diems* paid (in most, though not every, community), these often do not sufficiently compensate for time away from regular employment. Further, no amount of money is enough to compensate for time spent away from family.

And, while serving on a council can be linked to the ego needs of any individual, this should be of lesser significance than the sheer desire to be of help to others and to lead in the community. (Unfortunately, the ego factor can become predominant in seeking re-election, particularly after one or two terms.)

Public service is often a humbling experience. At its heart lies the willingness to make decisions on behalf of others based on a recognition that not all of these decisions will meet with the support of all residents. Indeed, there may be times that council makes a decision that brings out a considerable outpouring of negative comment.

When a council member is no longer concerned with what people think of his or her decisions and opinions, and when public criticism no longer stings, it is time to consider other ways to serve the community.

Openness to the Opinions of Others

One of the greatest challenges of any council member is not only understanding, but also accepting, the fact that the opinions of others may be in direct contradiction to one's own and, equally importantly, that those opinions may be more correct or appropriate. A successful member needs to be able to accept that there are likely to be very distinct differences of opinion around the council table. Such differences often ensure that the final decision is better balanced and more reflective of a broad cross-section of public views than would be the case within a council that thinks alike, or with one that believes all differences are to be muted.

Good decisions result from a healthy exchange of ideas and the sense that "my ideas are as valued as yours." Council members need to feel that their colleagues are genuinely interested in what they have to say on a topic. Being disrespectful in either word or actions (eg. body language and facial expressions) toward another member of council is not helpful to good decision making or to showing respect for public office.

The ability to handle differences with others is the mark of a mature mind. Our world includes many individuals with whom we might disagree on any number of subjects. Such disagreements should lead to a healthy discussion, based on a sharing of knowledge and opinions.

Case in Point

In one New Brunswick municipality, a member of council continually upset his colleagues by questioning the reports of the administration, as delivered to council via the chief administrative officer. While his questions were often quite reasonable, there always seemed to be an underlying message that the staff could not be trusted. This proved so irksome to one member that she spoke out loudly against her offending colleague and questioned his right to "attack" a member of staff without any evidence that the information was not complete or accurate. The councillor, who seemed to regularly offend the sensitivities of the others by his incessant questioning, was surprised by the response of his colleague and wondered aloud why he was under attack!

There are right and wrong ways to ask legitimate questions. There are also approaches that council members know will offend anyone with reasonable sensitivities. Holding off on asking the tough questions until the 11th hour (i.e. at a council meeting), when the question could have been asked during the day or over the weekend, is often a sign that the question was not the real issue: the opportunity to garner a front page comment based on a particularly aggressive or embarrassing exchange was.

Respect for Limitations of the Role

A member of council does not have unfettered authority. Becoming elected is not akin to being anointed. A council member who wants to make a contribution to the community needs to respect the legislated limits on his or her authority. Thus, no member of council should believe that he or she has the power to commit the municipality to any action, or to expend civic funds without an express and prior resolution of the council to do so.

It would be prudent of any council, at the outset of the term, to ensure that it has been provided with a clear overview of the legislation vis-a-vis conflict of interest (or pecuniary interest) and limits to personal power. If not understood, these related issues can undermine the effectiveness of any council and can, at times, lead to embarrassing and debilitating results. The difficulty can begin with members of council quickly realizing that their opinions are treated with more consideration since they have been elected than previously. Council members also perceive members of staff taking their suggestions seriously and actually trying to implement what might have been only idle musings by the member. Such suggestions (which have led to action by willing but misinformed staff) can soon become demands, with the result that a council becomes no better than its individual parts, because that is how it functions. The will of the body quickly is overshadowed by the insis-

31

tence of the individual. Before the council reaches this point, it is hoped that the CAO and mayor will call in external help, if necessary, to explain the rules of the game, and thereby create a culture that adheres to the legislation, and not to the "way we do business" mentality.

Case in Point

In one county, the mayor became concerned about the performance of a particular department head. The mayor contacted the municipality's solicitor and asked various questions regarding the municipality's options. These conversations occurred with increasing regularity over a five-month period without the knowledge of the council or the CAO. When the mayor appeared to abandon his pursuit of dismissal of the department head, the county's external legal counsel submitted an invoice. The CAO referred the matter to council, which eventually decided to pay the bill – but not before some heated discussions about the fact that the mayor overstepped his bounds in contacting the law firm without the council's express consent. Secondly, in doing so, the mayor also bypassed the CAO, whose contract (and the legislation) called for such authority to be limited to the CAO, not to an individual member of council.

Respect for Role of Administration

A council will only be successful to the extent that it understands that one of its principal duties is to develop a collegial relationship with its administration. A council member may think he or she is gaining a level of credibility by acting as the opposition to the administration through continuous attacks on both the reports, as well as the people presenting them. Such an assessment is wrong-headed and mistakes short-term media recognition with long-term progress on the community's key issues.

A successful council member works at developing professional relationships with the senior administration and a healthy degree of respect for their work. Such a relationship is based on recognition of the professionalism of senior staff and regard for their separate, distinct roles. It should not be confused with a desire for a personal friendship.

While such friendships can develop, it would be a lot more healthy if that were to blossom after the member had stepped down from office, rather than while still occupying a place on the council. The need for a relationship based on mutual respect between the member and administrator is far more important to the health of the community, and ought not to be sacrificed for a personal friendship that, while attractive in other circumstances, can become problematic in an employer-employee relationship.

The respect for the administration by a council member ought to be built on respect for the experience and academic preparation that such individuals bring to the table, and for their desire to serve the community. Such people are often hard to find, and can attract numerous offers from other communities and head-hunters based on their perceived expertise and quality service. The cost of replacing senior administrators can be considerable, and so some emphasis should be placed on developing a healthy relationship between council and the CAO, as discussed in greater detail in Chapter 11.

Case in Point

I have had the honour of being responsible for the recruitment of the first two chief administrative officers for the most northern capital city in Canada (Iqaluit) in our newest Territory of Nunavut. The cost to the community in hiring each was considerable, and included: travel for short-listed candidates; advertising (which the city tried unsuccessfully before seeking assistance); added costs for interim management between the date of departure of one officer; and the arrival of the new person; relocation costs for the new candidate; costs of recruitment advice; and the charges for legal counsel in the formulation of a contract. In addition, the council provides bonus provisions not found in other contracts, simply based on the northern location.

These costs are extensive. Thus, there is an inherent desire to retain the incumbent as long as that relationship is deemed to be acceptable. And, while the costs of recruitment to a southern community will be less, these are still significant. Further, the increased frequency of having to recruit to a senior level position does not go unnoticed by the administration marketplace. This tends to send signals that the basis of relationships between the council and senior staff may not be healthy, regardless of who holds the position.

Willingness to Challenge Administration

Regardless of this need for each council to develop a healthy degree of respect and trust in their administration, it needs to be equally clear that such respect is not based on a lack of questioning or an unwillingness to challenge. There may be several instances in any meeting of council or a committee of council wherein the report of administration is before council members and considerable disagreement arises. The argument may be over a philosophical position (do we charge user fees or don't we?) or it may be simply a disagreement as to the options presented or recommended by the CAO. It is incumbent upon a council member,

A GOOD COUNCILLOR HAS ...

- ☑ A willingness to serve other
- ☑ Openness to the opinions of others
- ☑ Respect for limitations of the role
- ☑ Respect for role of administration
- ☑ A willingness to challenge administration
- ☑ Enhanced sense of personal integrity
- ☑ Willingness to make decisions in a fishbowl
- ☑ Commitment to preparation
- ☑ Desire to be a leader
- ☑ Maturity
- ☑ Accountability
- ☑ Commitment to learning
- ☑ Focus on Community – Not On Single Group or Issue
- ☑ A willingness to ask dumb questions
- ☑ A willingness to accept democracy

having read a background report and questioning its conclusions, to contact the CAO (or department head in question) and ask a few questions regarding the rationale, and whether or not all of the key and available information has been considered. After having given the CAO the courtesy of hearing the concerns on a particular report, the council member is, or should be, at liberty to present his or her views to those present at a meeting, and to indicate why the report's findings are flawed or, in his or her opinion, not fully researched. If the options lack appropriate depth, or the report appears to be superficial in some way, a member of council should be comfortable in expressing those concerns.

The issue should never be one of reluctance to question the findings or conclusions of a report, but rather one of how best to make the point without causing personal embarrassment. Thus, commenting on the inadequacies of the report is appropriate; singling out a member of staff for verbal abuse is not.

Enhanced Sense of Personal Integrity

Norman Schwartzkopf, the military leader of the western nations in the 1991 Gulf War, is reported to have said that "leadership is a potent combination of strategy and integrity. If you must be without one, be without strategy." The underlying message here is the absolute need for all members of council to ensure that their actions are above reproach.

Contrary to what others have written on this topic, it is my view that it is not possible to effectively separate one's public and private roles. You cannot be a scoundrel in your business affairs and be continually before an investigative committee of the Stock Exchange, while concurrently presuming to occupy the moral high ground in questioning the ethics of the administration in accepting free trips to a southern destination for the purpose of assessing a new approach to managing hockey rinks.

Most people entering adult years should have a reasonably clear sense of what constitutes inappropriate behaviour. (I caveat this observation because my experience teaches me that it is equally apparent that some people do not grasp this, regardless of their age. I also recognize and admit that some of my personal choices in my earlier years were wrong or inappropriate and reflected poor judgment.) My experience, however, informs me that integrity is absolutely critical; a common understanding of what integrity means to a council is of considerable importance. Every member of council needs to gain an appreciation at the outset of a term of office, of what values and principles are important to their colleagues. This could be done in a council retreat/workshop, preferably with someone external to the council and administration facilitating the session (otherwise, it becomes another council meeting).

It is essential that each council member bring to the table a healthy concept of desired norms and values. Without that, consensus on meaningful issues is virtually impossible.

Case in Point

A Vancouver Island municipality requested a council retreat because the new council realized that they were immediately going to face several key issues that had a very strong potential to divide members and provoke considerable controversy. Because their predecessor council had developed a reputation for divisiveness throughout its term, this council wanted to see if another approach was possible.

Without getting into the actual issues they were going to face, we discussed the manner in which they wanted to approach tough issues, and the principles that they could follow in order to ensure a high degree of mutual respect without neutering the capacity of each to disagree on actual issues.

The proof will be in the pudding. However, the fact that this council was sufficiently proactive to even consider this approach, and the desire that they expressed to understand each other prior to taking their final positions on the topics indicated to me that they have a better than average chance of being successful.

Willingness to Make Decisions in a Fishbowl

Any person who commits to running for local office should understand that he or she will very quickly become involved in situations that require tough decisions to be made in the glare of the television cameras or in the spotlight of the local media. It does not take long after the election for someone new to local office to become acutely aware of the fact that certain decisions will result in the disfavour of one element of council or another, regardless of how well-researched the issue or how intensive the dialogue with the public.

The decisions of a council on public issues (with very few legislated exceptions) are to be made publicly. This general principle of local government has plagued many councils across Canada. Those elected on the promise of "open and transparent government" soon realize that, while the commitment sounds nice, the delivery is not so straightforward. There are issues that have considerable potential to be wrongly interpreted, or to be responded to negatively. There are issues that may upset your neighbour, and which you would prefer to make without that person sitting in front of you in the audience. While such issues may be *controversial*, that does not make them *confidential*. Holding a closed meeting to discuss the controversial issues is a sure-fire means of provoking the ire of the media and then the citizens. In addition, having a scheduled closed session before a council meeting (as opposed to after) is almost a guaranteed way to ensure that issues that are not legitimately confidential will be added to the agenda by an administration trying to protect its council from the eyes of the public.

Trying to eliminate the sense of "life in a fishbowl" is not possible for those in elected office. Whether it's making decisions in a council meeting, or shopping in a nearby city for goods or services that could be found in your own community, the actions of council members invite both scrutiny as well as comment. Those new to public life are wise to remember that an "off the record" conversation is best limited to one between spouses across the pillow – and preferably within your own home. If you find the notion of having to argue and then make tough decisions (on issues that will possibly have a negative impact on one element of the community or another) objectionable and something to be avoided at all costs, then stay out of politics at any level.

Commitment to Preparation

Anyone wanting to become successful in public life must commit considerable time for preparation. The degree of reading required by any member of council is often overwhelming. The idea that an elected official will only be expected to attend a council meeting every two weeks is based on false advertising. Council members serving communities ranging from the very small to mega-cities are generally inundated with background reports leading up to decisions by council (or by any number of associated boards and committees).

For every hour spent in the council chambers involved in making decisions, a council member is likely to spend at least another hour or two becoming familiar with the associated materials provided in the agenda package. It takes time for members to adequately prepare themselves for meetings, both in terms of reading the reports, and also highlighting those areas for question. Some may even proceed to draft their own alternative resolutions if the recommended solutions put before council by the administration are not deemed to be acceptable.

In some instances, a member may consider it necessary to check with the CAO or department head as to the rationale in drafting recommendations, or a member may simply want to verify certain information or present new information that may not have been previously considered. Council as a whole should agree to the protocol by which this is done, so that the time taken up by each member is not overly extensive, and so that members of the administration are cautioned about being overly compliant in responding to such requests or suggestions. Both of these precautions are important, and both have caught more than one member of senior staff from time to time.

Case in Point

In one southern Ontario community, members of council were divided philosophically in terms of planning issues (and virtually all other issues as well). Certain councillors had become used to "dropping in" on the senior planner or a member of his department to "discuss" planning issues. This discussion often either led to or had the effect of changing the opinions presented to the rest of council. As a result, there developed a clear perception that policy matters were beginning to reflect the will of factions of council, rather than being the best apolitical advice the planning department could offer.

The next election changed the councillor involved, and the CAO also removed the planning director and appointed one with strong professionalism and a spine of steel.

It's not that the council shouldn't have the opportunity to express concerns. But, there is a significant difference in asking questions, and leaning heavily on administrators who see the person in the office as someone who very likely could influence whether or not they have jobs a month later.

Desire to Be a Leader

Those who choose to serve their communities in positions of elected leadership need to be willing and prepared to lead. While this might seem self-evident, it is not always observable from the reactions and behaviour of individual members of council. Often, a member may feel more content with the status quo, and thus not challenge how the municipality delivers its business or question whether or not the "business" of the municipality is appropriate given the current circumstances. As some wag once remarked, "A conclusion is the place where you got tired of thinking." Based on that adage, it becomes clear that certain people are all too willing to jump to conclusions. Sometimes that's appropriate; sometimes it's not.

For my own part, I have a tendency to be action-oriented. I want to quickly size up a matter and then move to its resolution. My style is tempered by those near and dear to me. As but one example, we have a young friend who is blind, and with whom we spend time whenever our mutual schedules permit. When we go out for a meal, he wants to know what is on the menu before choosing. I, on the other hand want to get past the meal selection and onto other matters of discussion. And so, I generally remark, "Look, there are only three choices on the menu." And I proceed to rattle off three obvious choices, hoping of course that he will select one (but realizing that this never works, and so the fun continues). He will turn knowingly to my wife and request her assistance in knowing what options are available.

Both styles reflect differing ways of approaching leadership – and both can work under the right circumstances. My style is likely more suited to the fire department, which generally does not have much leeway in terms of deciding to pass the hose. The latter style would likely work better if various planning options are on the table for consideration.

Case in Point

When I presented the council of a newly formed Ontario municipality with a model of governance that had not, to my understanding, been used before in any other city in Canada, I first asked if the council was prepared to be leaders. Everyone responded in the affirmative. I asked if they were prepared to try something different. I placed a caveat on my remarks by saying that what I eventually presented would not be illegal. Everyone seemed to be in agreement, and may have been caught up in the excitement of beginning a new venture.

When the model was unveiled, the first question (you guessed it) was "who else does things this way?!" (As it turned out, they were right to question the newly minted governance model because they saw the need to alter it later to better suit their emerging circumstances.)

Maturity

It should be evident that those holding elected office need to exercise maturity in their actions, comments and decision making. Unfortunately, this is all too often not the norm. While it would be encouraging to report that great progress is being made in raising the bar of conduct in governance, it would also be false – at least based on my observations of councils across Canada.

Our council chambers tend to reflect our society. And, while we have more people than ever taking further education courses or becoming better educated, the level of education does not appear to generate an increased level of maturity and decency. The lack of respect that we see in so many forums and media today is also reflected in the way members of council interact with each other, the public and the administration.

A mature member of council is able to keep the focus on the issues and away from personalities. He or she refuses to engage in mean-spirited dialogue and remarks designed to undermine others; seeks to understand the position being placed before council by a delegation, even when the point appears to be repeated or when the presenter has spoken previously (and to no avail) on much the same topic; and respects the administration and their efforts to serve both the community and council.

Commitment to Learning

Becoming an elected official is not as simple as being elected. This is an entirely new role for anyone entering public life and, as a result, there ought to be an expectation of the need for ongoing learning. The alternative sentiment might be described as follows: "I didn't know what this was all about when I started and I plan to leave with the same degree of understanding! I'm here to save the people some money.

Why would I want to spend it on becoming more learned or more effective?"

There is a lot to learn for someone is serious about developing skills as an elected official in order to add value to the community. Each province has an association of municipalities whose mandate includes enhancing the understanding of the role of an elected official. The Federation of Canadian Municipalities also incorporates seminars into their annual conferences and seminars that add clarity and breadth to the role of a local government elected official. The costs of such training are not exorbitant when one considers the scale of municipal budgets. If properly presented to the populace, the rationale for such training is readily understood, as long as it is not abused.

Attending conferences so as to see another city at the taxpayers' expense is not acceptable. Leaving sessions early to do a little shopping with the spouse is not likely to earn the applause of the sceptical taxpayer either. Attending with the sole focus of becoming better equipped to do the work of the residents at home is both sustainable and affordable, however. Thus, if an elected official is serious about learning more and becoming more effective in the process, there are opportunities to do so, and these should be pursued.

Accountability

"The buck stops here!" Most of us have either heard that line or have used it in one context or another. In the main, it refers to the quaint notion that someone is actually responsible for decisions made and actions taken. Thus, regardless of whether the advice on which council acted came from the CAO or from another source, any decision made by council is ... council's. Standing up and being counted – even when there is opposition to a decision – is far preferable and more likely to gain you public acclaim than deferring the accountability to the administration (or others).

Elected officials need to recognize the public's respect for those who admit to a poor decision, or who are prepared to shoulder the blame when, in truth, much of it might rightfully fall someplace else. Life is not always or only about taking credit for the sunshine. Standing up to a barrage of criticism for a decision that turns out to be premature or faulty in some regard is a hallmark of an honest and courageous politician. Caving in at the first sign of difficulty is weakness and cowardice personified.

Focus on Community — Not On Single Group or Issue

Far too frequently, council members speak and act as though they were representing only a segment of the community. In many parts of Canada, the legislation clearly states that the members of council are to represent the whole community regardless of whether or not they have been elected by a "ward" or "division." Even those who are elected by wards cannot be truly effective if their main focus is on a particular geographic area, while disregarding the whole.

Further, members of council need to ensure that they are fully engaged on all issues, not just those that they favour or on which they campaigned. The community is not well-served if a portion of its council sees its mandate as representing and only being interested in environmental concerns, rather than paying attention to economic issues as well. Most people that are able to engage the breadth of their minds recognize that issues impact the local economy, regardless of whether or not they pertain to saving forested areas or developing new recreation facilities. Most also recognize that saving natural areas is good business and good for the well-being of the community.

Ask "Dumb" Questions

The notion of "asking the dumb question" has been ascribed to Peter Drucker, the revered management guru who passed away recently at 95, after a long and very productive life. His philosophy was that any question that came to mind during an examination of agenda matters was legitimate, and likely on the minds of others as well. For that reason alone, argued Drucker, one ought to voice their question and allow others to join in the discussion.

Most of us feel somewhat inadequate on one or more topics. We cannot be well-versed on all, nor are we likely to even be interested in some. Any council meeting might involve discussions on major financial issues, new construction projects, social services, provincial policy, by-laws that are written in the prescribed manner (such that only the most experienced – or those with legal training – seem competent to understand), and so on. The only way a member of council can expect to fully comprehend the issues facing council is to ask whatever questions appear to be appropriate at that moment. (If such questions come to mind during the time prior to a meeting of council or committee of council, then council members ought to be encouraged to contact the senior administration for clarification prior to the actual council meeting.) A written protocol should be developed that provides clarification to this process so that council members can be assured that: (a) they are doing the right thing; and (b) the responses to their questions will be circulated to all members of council on a concurrent basis.

It is important that council and the administration discuss at the outset of any term of office the appropriateness of seeking clarification on issues where the council member has some uncertainty. Even if the member feels obliged to raise the issue in a public forum, if the administration are given advance notice of the issue, there is far less likelihood of it being perceived as an attempt to simply embarrass the staff.

Accept Democracy

Successful councils both recognize and appreciate the value of functioning within a democracy. Our system enables the public to elect those it deems most likely to act in an honest, ethical fashion as their representatives. Our local governments are also based on a rule of law and legal precedents that provide the framework within which the administration is able to function.

A successful council member must understand that he or she will not always be on the winning side of council's decisions, and must be gracious enough to accept that fact. Regardless of how strongly a member of council feels about an issue, a majority of their colleagues may feel otherwise. And, while each member should exercise all of their skills in trying to present an issue within the legitimate constraints of the procedural by-law and the legislation, the matter should be considered closed once the council makes its decision. Trying to bring new issues to the table in support of the argument after the decision has already been made is unlikely to sway the opinions of other members of council, *unless* the information is dramatically at odds with whatever was in the possession of council at the time of its decision.

It is unfortunate that, all too frequently, council members are fully supportive of the adage "four beats three" – until they find themselves on the losing side. If the council debated the matter; if the information provided by the administration reflected their best effort to succinctly address the matter; if questions were responded to as completely as possible; and if no information was being deliberately withheld, it might be safely assumed, in the vast majority of such instances, that the public would have voted in the same manner. It is called democracy.

Chapter 7

ORIENTATION TO GOVERNANCE IS CRITICAL

Whenever called in to examine difficult situations, I try to track back to where the issues began. History often reveals a lot about how the council and administration got into a mess, and may help identify some of the building blocks in terms of getting the ship of state righted again. Invariably, I find that either the council received no orientation at all ("we were only replacing three of the council members") or that the orientation was largely one of "this is how we, as the administration, run the place." In either or both instances, the problems lie in the process.

Case in Point

A community in the Maritimes was struggling in terms of the linkage between the council and the CAO. It was apparent that the relationship had soured between the mayor and some members of council, and now the two camps within council were trying to gain the CAO as "their" ally.

When I was called in, I asked to see the briefing binder that had been prepared for all members of council. As a result of what I was given (rather reluctantly by the clerk), I made two observations: one, the briefing session was only scheduled for the new members of council, and then those were done one-on-one; and two, nowhere in the briefing was time scheduled for discussing the CAO-council relationship. This was felt to be something that simply evolved over time, as though by some process of osmosis.

Like any new "employee" of an organization, most new members of council come to the table expecting to be briefed on all they need to know so as to function effectively. In many instances, however, they arrive unaware of the background orientation materials that exist. The lack of awareness of previous actions or decisions on related matters serves only to handicap new council members who would have benefited from access to the historical backdrop. Even when they sense additional materials may exist, they may be somewhat uncertain about appearing to be too demanding at the outset of their term.

Many council members I have met over the years are not particularly demanding, and thus may not be comfortable admitting that they don't fully understand their new role. While some administrators may ignore the real value of comprehensive council orientations by design, most of the others fail to adequately orient their new leaders by benign neglect. Past practice is often relied upon, and age-old orientation schedules are brought forward (often by the clerk's office); dusted off; new names inserted; and various players (largely, if not exclusively, internal administrative staff) are requested to participate in a half- or one-day orientation program.

The Problem With Most Orientations

Why is this not acceptable? There are several reasons. First, the orientation is treated as a "day-timer" item. That is, this is simply one of many "things" on a "to do" list carefully constructed over the years by administrations, by provincial-municipal organizations and municipal affairs departments, upon whom most practitioners rely. As a result, the reason for doing so is flawed, and generally, so too are the results. The process itself may be suitable, and the topics to be covered may appear comprehensive, but the focus needed by those governing is often absent.

Second, the emphasis of many orientations planned for new councils is often skewed towards the administration's view of what is important, and not that of the council. Thus, council may be treated to an hour of briefing on the role of council ("you set the policies"; "we, the administration, manage within those policies") and then the rest of the day is given over to an extensive overview of what each department does, sometimes with a tour of the municipality thrown in for good measure.

Third, the emphasis of some orientations is on what is legally permissible, and what is not. This approach is meant to separate the wheat from the chaff. If a council member still feels keen to continue with their new role after being advised of the imminent prospect of legal action against them and their heirs, it is apparent you have a keeper! The theme running throughout such sessions (based on personal experience, and with all due respect to my colleagues in the legal profession) is "What can go wrong from a legal standpoint, and how not to step on too many landmines." Inadvertently, the message becomes, "Take no stand until you have checked out all the legal consequences." With tongue in cheek, this makes for steady work for the legal community.

New members of council are often at a significant disadvantage unless they are afforded access to a first-rate, carefully planned orientation, targeted at their roles. While new members of council require a briefing on the logistical aspects of their new lives, it is the absence of any real focus on their actual roles that causes much of the difficulty in separating the roles of council from that of the administration. The focus of the orientation should not be on how the internal system functions. If that is a necessary component, schedule that for day two. Now, what do you suppose ought to be the focus of day one?

Key Elements of a Comprehensive Council Orientation

Municipalities have historically mishandled orientations by placing the emphasis on the wrong message, and by presuming that elected officials actually had a clear grasp of the basic fundamentals of being an elected official before they ran for office. Further, the fact that someone has already served one or more terms is misinterpreted so as to mean that that individual has grasped a solid understanding of the role in his or her prior term(s) of office. This misunderstanding is not due to any deliberate neglect or avoidance of the real issues. It is simply a matter of not knowing what is expected by an elected official or what would make a substantive difference in how he or she performed in the new role.

There are two basic reasons for such failures: one is the inability to answer the simple yet fundamental question: What is "governance"? The supplementary reason is the inability to understand or think through the question: What do council members need to understand in order to add value to the leadership of our community?

Without a solid grasp of the fundamentals of governance by those involved in any orientation, the recipients of the training often come to a grossly inadequate understanding of what it means to be a member of council. This is not to say that such recipients cannot become effective as members of council. Rather, it is that they do so in spite of their original orientation, not as a natural consequence.

Council Members Need ...

In some provinces, members of council are sworn in as the new council almost immediately after the election. The organizational meeting (to confirm or re-establish or revise meeting dates, committee appointments and other matters of protocol) is held within a week or two of the election. In other provinces, the outgoing council is required to hold office for a period of about two weeks, during which it may hold at least one more regular council meeting, presumably so as to conclude any leftover business. While the former approach would appear to make more sense in a number of ways, both approaches leave very little time for a new council to "hit the ground running."

So, what does a member of council need to understand in order to become sufficiently familiar with the new role as quickly as possible? The following (summarized in the Orientation Agenda on the opposite page) will not appear in legislated form, nor even perhaps in a procedural by-law. Nevertheless, these aspects are integral to a successful term.

Essence of Leadership

Some degree of training is needed on what it means to actually lead issues and a community. Leaders lead. They set the course. As many writers and scholars have previously noted, leadership is not management. The former has more to do with what needs to be done, whereas the latter tends to deal more with how best to get it done (in what order, with what personnel, by what time, using what resources, from what source, and so on).

It is my observation that the reason so many people fail at community leadership is that they simply do not understand the notion of leadership. Perhaps they have not had to be involved in performing leadership functions in a similar capacity, or perhaps they perceive that their principal task is to approve the recommended actions of the administration. Unfortunately, there are few opportunities to develop leadership skills in a similar setting, as very few leadership development courses or training institutes equate with the challenges of acting as leaders in a local government setting.

Leadership is not simply about reducing the budget for this or that item or approving the minutes of this committee or that. Such tasks do not require much leadership. Leaders step up to a different level than many of those whom they lead. They ask penetrating questions; they search for new ideas and alternatives; they question the status quo, rather than blindly accepting that all avenues for resolution have been tried. Leaders see what needs to be done, and they set about putting the wheels in motion to make it happen. They see before others do, and they have the courage to act on their convictions.

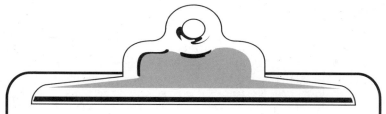

ORIENTATION AGENDA

Elected officials need an orientation that allows them to understand:

- ☑ Essence of Leadership

- ☑ A Servant Mindset

- ☑ Clarity as to Role

- ☑ Understanding How to Build Consensus

- ☑ Guidance in Putting Forward Motions

- ☑ Know the Rules of Procedure

- ☑ How and When to Access the Administration

- ☑ Handling Calls and Correspondence from the Public

- ☑ Using the Decision-Making Process of Council

- ☑ Understanding the Impact of Present Policy

- ☑ Role of Media: Avoiding a Breach of Confidentiality Obligations

- ☑ Linkage to the Public

- ☑ What Use of Civic Resources is Appropriate?

- ☑ Current Key Issues (i.e. History, Current Status)

- ☑ How, Why and When We Get Paid

Leaders stand up. They recognize a problem as an opportunity to make something better. They refuse to simply see obstacles. Issues that need to be resolved are resolved. If a difficult and potentially unpopular stance needs to be articulated, they can say it. If the heat on a decision turns up, so too does their resolve. If the decision of the council is right in light of present circumstances, it can and will be defended.

A Servant Mindset

By its nature, elected life often attracts those who have a higher sense of self worth than many of their contemporaries. They seldom show much sign of weakness or helplessness, and use various techniques to cover up any sense of inferiority or inadequacy that they might feel. Many are very good at communicating their own views and positions, and somewhat less patient with those who do not ascribe to similar views.

Other elected officials would likely accept the foregoing description as true. At the same time, they recognize that, in order to be successful as an elected official, one needs to have a great desire to be of service to others. Leading the public can be akin, at times, to pushing a string uphill. The process can be tedious and quite often thankless. At the same time, elected officials realize their need to act in a compassionate manner towards others, and always be open to hearing their concerns and complaints. The need for a servant's heart is based on the belief that public service is simply that: a willingness to put the needs of others before your own welfare.

This notion of serving others works wonders in terms of reducing any sense of haughtiness or "I'm above it all" attitude. Service to others can be a humbling experience. It is not all about the glory of public office. It is the small things that are done to ease the stress on others that provide the sense of gratification in the life of most politicians. When that ceases to be the case, an exit from political life is highly recommended!

Clarity as to Role

An orientation program should be offered for each new council (and all the members elected to it) based on the philosophy that this indeed is an important and distinct role. Any presumption that those elected fully understand their role would be a colossal mistake. Unless the administration of a municipality wants to spend the majority of its time re-educating the council, being proactive by planning a comprehensive, pragmatic overview of the roles and responsibilities of elected officials is highly recommended.

All too often, those conducting orientation sessions fail to recognize that their audience of new members of council does not necessarily comprehend what those instructing may take for granted. That is, there are very clear distinctions between what administrators do and what elected officials do. Either those charged with leading such training sessions suffer from the fond hope that something this simple does not need to be clarified, or they may feel that having to spend much time clarifying roles might sound patronizing.

Assuming that all those elected to office realize that their role is substantially different from those administering the business of the municipality is a quantum and often-tragic mistake.

A solid orientation ensures that considerable time is spent focusing on the nature of these differences.

Understanding How to Build Consensus

Council members need to be trained in the art of consensus building. For many strong-willed people, this unique ability does not come easily. Good decisions, however, are generally not the result of one person crafting the "right" answer, but rather the combination of the thoughts of many. Consensus decision making requires a comprehensive understanding of the reports from the administration, together with additional input into the process as a result of committee deliberations and hallway discussions.

While the mayor has an obligation to determine if there is any room for negotiation or compromise, other members of council can also assist in identifying and clarifying options and potential resolutions. Generally speaking, one of the best opportunities for issues to be discussed and other options explored is found in committee meetings. Those attending are generally less fixed in their views and open to suggested approaches that might "work." Committee meetings present forums for discussion and debate, and tend to be far less formal and less adversarial than a council meeting.

A thorough orientation session should include a briefing on how decisions are made and where consensus seems to be most acceptable and productive in the local context.

Guidance in Putting Forward Motions

I have dealt with some members of council who have advised that they spent a whole term, or most of one, reluctant to make a motion for fear that it would not come out right and they would be embarrassed by the result. Placing a motion before the rest of council is, in most communities, the only way new business gets done. There are various ways that this is accomplished.

In some communities, the administration may be called on to draft virtually all the required resolutions and "assign" proposed resolutions to members of council based on some form of rotation, a committee responsibility, or on the basis of a particular interest on the topic.

In others, a member of council may simply move the recommendation put forward by the CAO. Alternatively, a member of council may draft their own resolution on an issue, because the options as determined by the administration are not deemed to be acceptable.

In some instances, matters of limited consequence or those that were endorsed by a committee of council may be put forward through a "consent agenda." By using this mechanism, a council can approve a series of recommendations in one motion by moving adoption of the consent agenda.

The ability to place a motion before the council can be restricted by the procedural by-law. This may limit members to serving a notice of motion in order to have a matter addressed, or it may allow members to place items before an agenda committee of council who will consider the merits of a recommended request or report.

In some cases, the intent of restricting councillors' freedom in what to place before council and when is predicated on the desire to shield members of the administration from frivolous or vexatious requests, or to ensure that no item is to be considered that has not already been referred to the administration for research and comment.

An issue as seemingly straightforward as placing a motion before council can prove perplexing to new members of council. As a courtesy, the administration should provide pragmatic advice to every new council member on how to get their items of concern to the attention of the whole council. The current mechanism must be understood by every member of council, regardless of whether or not they ever make a motion that is solely of their own making. Seasoned staff could either provide the training themselves, or bring in a reputable parliamentarian who understands how a local government system works.

Know the Rules of Procedure

Part and parcel of developing motions is developing a solid understanding of how the business of council is to be done according to the approved procedural by-law. All members of council ought to be trained on the requirements of their by-law and what steps are necessary to have a matter considered and approved. Most procedural by-laws include the legislated requirements, as well as "rules of order" defining how motions are placed, amended, rescinded, lost or approved. The requirements for by-law readings are also identified, as are various other specifications for conducting the business of council. These are very important guidelines for the conduct of council's business, and can affect how and when decisions are made.

Equally important is the need for council members to recognize when their meetings and decision making are hindered by the constraints imposed by a procedural by-law. Some by-laws are overly lengthy or wordy, or are written in a manner that only a parliamentary expert would grasp. The by-law is a tool of council for ensuring that decisions are made according to a particular framework whereby all members of council are afforded both protection and direction equal to others. Where it negates good decision making, the onus is on council to request a review of the by-law to determine which clauses are essential, and those which have simply been added to deal with issues and conditions that may no longer apply.

Case in Point

A member of a council in southern Alberta is notorious for finding every way imaginable to obstruct the conduct of council's business and, in particular, to make the senior administration look inept and lacking confidence. The councillor asks loaded questions and continues to ask, even once quite suitable and comprehensive answers are rendered. No one escapes his ire and the media loves his antics, while protesting regularly to the contrary.

A new mayor is elected who is determined to afford his administration more protection from his nemesis on council. He convinces his colleagues to amend the procedural by-law to restrict members of council from asking more than one question on any topic. While this addresses the repetitive nature of the councillor's antics, the provision restricts the ability of the rest of council to ask useful follow-up questions.

The council is now noted as being more polite, but not necessarily more effective.

How and When to Access the Administration

One of the useful aspects of a logistics briefing during the course of an orientation program is clarification on how members of council are to access the administration. Depending on the size and sometimes the experience of a council, the degree of access may be very open or particularly closed. At the end of the day, neither approach works very well. One school of thought suggests that no constraints should be placed on such access; other municipalities, however, have found it necessary to place very rigorous limits on access to the administration, given the abuse of this by prior councils or by individual members of council.

In smaller communities, the tendency by some is to go directly to the person who is seen to be in charge of (or most knowledgeable about) the matter in question. This is justified as being the simplest and most direct approach to getting an answer for the ratepayer, but is also just as often abused. Staff members may be harangued by a council member into accepting an answer or direction that has not been prescribed by council nor by current policy. In many instances, council members use this technique to "get the gospel." Others bypass the structure so as to undermine the role and rights of the chief administrative officer (or a particular department head they may not respect).

A written protocol needs to be established that defines, at least in broad terms, the steps a member is to follow in:

➤ trying to access staff in order to find out information;

➤ getting action started as a result of a citizen's complaint;

➤ seeking advice to respond to a citizen's inquiry;

➤ finding additional background information on a particular matter; and

➤ becoming better informed in advance of a council or committee meeting.

In the absence of such a protocol, council members may be inclined to take whatever steps they feel appropriate to get to the information they feel they need to make an informed decision. While some experienced members like this approach (and may resent any questioning of their strategies), this is generally unsuitable and unfair. Leaving the nature of the approach to an individual member can result in:

➤ wasted energies (a number of council members call the same employee on the same issue);

➤ some council members having much better access than others;

➤ misinformation from junior staff being circulated as though it were the approved municipal policy;

➤ other levels of employees being undermined as the structure is bypassed;

➤ the CAO having little idea as to the nature of the requests or concerns of members of council; and

➤ an inability to track whether or not the follow-up information was suitable and comprehensive.

Handling Calls and Correspondence From the Public

Related to the foregoing is the need to provide members of council with advice on how to handle direct contacts with members of the public. Every member of council will receive calls from constituents seeking answers to all manner of issues and questions. Without clear guidance as to what is appropriate and what is not, such matters may be answered in ways that are contradictory or that give the appearance of an approval when, in fact, only council has the authority to bind the full council and to direct the administration (through the CAO).

Some basic guidelines to follow should include:

➤ Keep a pen and notebook, or electronic device, handy in order to record the names and phone numbers of those seeking answers or who pass along complaints.

➤ Commit only to passing the issue along to the most appropriate person for a response.

➤ Assure the complainant that the staff are committed to service excellence, and you are certain that all complaints will be quickly and appropriately handled.

➤ Ask the caller to contact you again within 10 days (if that is appropriate) if they have not received a satisfactory answer by then.

➤ Respond to all calls (practise courtesy).

➤ Respond to all emails and letters within seven days, even if just to acknowledge receipt.

Using the Decision-Making Process of Council

Council members need to understand the steps that are normally followed in any decision-making process. The orientation should include a comprehensive description of the process including:

► steps to resolution from the outset of an issue being raised;

► research role of staff in determining how it should be resolved;

► role of a department head in determining if the issue lies outside of current policy or within his or her authority to approve;

► development of a "request for decision" through which the issue is presented to the CAO and possibly the management team; and

► determination by the CAO on whether the issue is to go before council for resolution.

Council members should also be advised on what basis an issue might be referred to a committee or agency of council; what that process entails; and when council would normally be expected to give the issue its final approval.

Council members should also be advised as to the mandate of any committees and boards and how these relate to the decision-making process, as well as how to place items on the committee agenda.

Understanding the Impact of Present Policy

Members of council need to know that those policies and by-laws presently "on the books" will be adhered to by the administration unless they are specifically directed otherwise by a resolution of council. It is interesting, therefore, that so little attention is devoted to a critical examination of what policies currently exist, and the impact that those policies have on how the administration responds to requests from the public. Ironically, some people run for office because they are opposed to what they perceive as the policies of the current council. Having made considerable noise over their displeasure, they then fail to bring up this matter with their colleagues or the administration, thereby proving that the policies were not the issue, becoming elected was.

Role of Media: Avoiding a Breach of Confidentiality Obligations

The media's role is to produce information that they feel will be of interest to their readers or viewers. Their job is not to advertise the issues that council thinks are important. A leading member of the Vancouver media once said to me, "Our job is to report the unusual." And, it's true; that is generally what they report. "Man chews up pit bull" rates the front page, complete with pictures. "Pit bull chews man" may still be news, but is more likely to be found relegated to page five.

Invariably, one or more members of council will misunderstand the role of the media, and decide to share some confidential information with the media in order to make a point, or to gain their trust. Just as quickly, the council member in question loses the confidence of his or her fellow members on council. (And, often just as quickly, the media releases the information provided as a public service!)

There are generally very good reasons behind council protocols, including those that pertain to how information is to be released. Regardless of the temptation and the "logic" of sharing information that has been clearly identified as confidential, no member of council is above the law, nor should any feel inclined to operate outside of council's authorization. Items that are identified as "confidential" are presumably so marked because they fall within the parameters of confidential issues that the legislation dictates. If the matter is in dispute as to whether or not it is truly confidential, the municipality's solicitor should be consulted by the CAO and the opinion, preferably in writing, presented to the council as a whole. (If a member wants to challenge the matter, then that discussion should also be held in closed session.)

If the resolve of council is that the matter ought to remain confidential, then anyone in the minority on that issue needs to show confidence in their fellow council members and agree to accept the will of the majority. (It is easy to be a strong advocate of democracy when you are on the winning side of the vote.)

Linkage to the Public

Politicians are elected as a result of their ability to connect with others in society. They generally exude a mixture of confidence and sincerity. They empower others, and they receive power from others. They build up, and they draw in. In short, they connect where others are at. Most have a "can do" spirit that often translates into action, and tend to be seeking solutions while others are still wringing their hands over the problems.

Much of their energy is derived from their contact with others. Seldom are political leaders reclusive or shrinking violets. Most love to mix. Like public speakers, they've never met a microphone they did not like! While others in society stay back when the issues become heated, political leaders jump in because they know the answers (or think they know).

Local elected officials need to maintain their contacts with the public. While this should be obvious, sometimes elected officials begin to believe that their primary audience is in city hall. That is where they gravitate to, and that is where they sense the power of their office. Unfortunately, the source of that power is not city hall – it's the people who are in the community, and who put people into city hall for a period of time to do their bidding.

A thorough orientation process needs to include reminders of this fact. It needs to encourage elected officials to stay connected by being visible in the community, by attending events, by visiting the friends they had before becoming elected, by giving a voice to those who feel that "city hall" does not listen.

What Use of Civic Resources is Appropriate?

Civic resources are public resources. The notepads at the municipal office are there for the use of elected officials while doing work on behalf of the community. The communication systems (telephone, fax, email, etc.) are there for the use of elected officials doing public business. These resources are not there to supplement one's own business endeavours, or to provide family members with their school supplies.

Similarly, unless staff have been hired directly for an individual council member in a large centre, civic employees work for the public, not for individual elected officials. Accessing their help on a matter is often legitimate provided that the established protocol is followed (i.e. check with the CAO or relevant department head before proceeding, not after). Expecting a staff member to write up a report, or to attend with the member to a community meeting, or to visit a neighbour whose garbage stinks, or whose used cars are lying all over the yard, are not normally considered matters of public interest. Simply because historical matters are a favourite issue of an individual member, they are not necessarily topics on which that member is entitled to seek the assistance of staff members. Unless the matter has been referred to a committee on which the member serves, or is guided by a department head under whose jurisdiction the matter lies, the interest in such matters is the member's alone. Thus, asking for staff assistance is not appropriate.

Council members should be reminded as to the protocol to follow with respect to their contacts with staff members. Otherwise, this can become a very difficult matter.

Current Key Issues(i.e. History and Current Status)

New members of council should also expect to receive a thorough briefing by the administration on any outstanding, ongoing issues of importance. This will ensure that each new member is up to speed on the issues in relation to the returning members, and thus better able to debate the matters on an equal basis. (While this may not be possible because of the rich history that some issues have, and that might only be understood through having sat through the debates at council, the intent of the administration should always be to move everyone to a similar starting post.)

A goal of the orientation should be to ensure that the learning curve is as smooth as possible, and that the time to become familiar with the issue, as well as the process of governance, is reduced. The aim, of course, should be to have each member up to speed as quickly as possible in terms of understanding their role and their new milieu.

The notion that new council members should be groomed for their roles by a returning member of council ought to be disavowed. Every member of a council assumes office having access to the same rights and privileges as their colleagues. The notion of two tiers of council members is contrary to the notion of all being created (or elected) equal. Having any returning members volunteer to spend time with new members should be welcomed. Institutionalizing that measure, however, creates an ill-conceived dependency, and gives weight to the flawed notion of returning members assuming a predominant role on the prime committees.

Citizens are not asked to elect returning versus new members of council. They are asked: "Who best to serve us?" Any action or inference that one member of council has prerogatives not enjoyed by others is foolish and misdirected.

How, Why and When We Get Paid

The issue of council compensation is delicate and should therefore be approached with due caution. It has caused many communities to rise up against a council that dared to raise their own salaries mid-stream without the opportunity for the public to comment. Any council policy on the matter of compensation for council members needs to take into account the following components.

Significance of the office of mayor – The mayor's position must be recognized as the core of the leadership team. With that must be acknowledged the need for additional time spent "on the job." There needs to be an understanding that the mayor's position may well be more than part-time, particularly if the mayor is expected to represent the municipality on external bodies. While it may be possible for a mayor to maintain another occupation, it is obvious that there will be substantial time requirements imposed by the role of the mayor in this capacity. That person needs considerable flexibility in order to accommodate the demands of the position. This is generally deemed to be a position of importance and the epitome of the volunteer sector. As a result, some of the time spent by the mayor is perceived as just that, "volunteering." By the same token, the municipality benefits from the mayor developing significant external contacts with the other levels of government, leaders of the Federation of Canadian Municipalities, and the provincial association of municipalities.

Importance of the role of councillor – The position of councillor (or alderman as it is designated in some communities) is also very important and can be advantageous to the community in terms of the calibre of leadership being provided. There are many demands placed on individual members of council and the time expectations of this role are often very burdensome to anyone with a career or other full-time occupation, including that of spouse, parent or principal breadwinner. These are important roles given the leadership these people bring to the local community, and the authority that a council has to make rather significant decisions.

Voluntary nature – There needs to be common recognition that a portion of the time spent in these roles is expected to be of a voluntary nature. It is difficult to account for all of the time a member of council spends in such roles, and thus some of this time ought to be considered as a voluntary contribution to the community.

Honoraria – Council honoraria, paid to councillors and the mayor on a monthly basis, is provided in recognition of the regular demands of the position in terms of the regular meetings of council, any committee or board meetings in the municipality, and any time needed to prepare for meetings, including touring an area or visiting a resident/business. Time taken to respond to emails and other forms of correspondence are also considered when establishing the council's honoraria. In some jurisdictions, one-third of the remuneration to be paid to council members is to be a non-accountable allowance for expenses incurred for council-related business, other than those expenses already covered by council's current compensation by-law.

Council per diems – On the other hand, any time taken beyond the normal duties expected of a council member in terms of municipal meetings – such as attendance at a local council one-day retreat, or attendance at the provincial association's conference, or one of their sponsored seminars – should be considered as beyond the scope of council monthly honoraria. These days or portions thereof should be paid a per diem in accordance with the schedule established for such purposes. An annual budget should be set for this purpose and should be capped such that each member of council is made aware of what they are allowed to charge for per diems in each year of a council term. Council members should not be expected to sacrifice their holidays to be a member of council. Any conferences or seminars that have received the pre-approval of council should be attended by one or more members, and the costs for that, including a reasonable per diem, should be the obligation of the municipality. A municipality should allow a maximum of 10-15 days for any member attending conferences or seminars on the pre-authorization of council, either by a policy or pre-approved list of such attendances at the beginning of each year.

Expenses – Expenses are established by policy and cover those costs and incidentals that a council member incurs as a consequence of acting on behalf of the community in this role. Council members should be provided with a flat rate for monthly travel within the municipality and its immediate environment (say 30 km). Any travel beyond these parameters (eg. for a course or a conference held further afield) should be paid at a separate rate that has been established on an annual basis. If air travel is necessary, flight costs should be based on the best rate available and by receipt only. Any incidentals such as taxis should be at cost and by receipt. The policy relative to meal expenses should be reasonable based on regional standards, and should be incurred for meals that were necessitated as a part of the council's business. Accommodation costs should be based on a reasonable allowance or by direct billing at a family-level establishment. The per diem rate should be adjusted annually on January 1 of each year by an amount equal to the change in the Consumer Price Index for the region in which the municipality is located. All expense accounts submitted by a member of council should be reviewed and signed for approval by the mayor and one other member of council (preferably someone not involved in the same claim if possible). All expense claims submitted by the mayor must be reviewed by the deputy mayor and one other member of council.

Regular reviews – A process ought to be established that would see regular reviews of council honoraria and expenses by a citizens' committee every three to four years (depending on the length of a council term – which, incidentally, I believe should be fixed across Canada at four years. The committee should be comprised of those people whose legitimacy would be difficult to assail, even by the most inquisitive and mean-spirited individuals. The committee's report should be adopted within 90 days before any subsequent election, and should be slated for implementation the day following the next election (thereby negating the charge that a council is simply feathering its own nest).

Conclusion

The list of topics on the orientation agenda is not a short one – nor is it a simple one. By paying attention to these issues and establishing a focus at the outset of the term for the new council, though, the size (and frequency) of stumbling blocks encountered later can be greatly minimized. Proper orientation is essential to good local governance.

Chapter 8

JOB DESCRIPTION: COUNCIL, MAYOR, COUNCILLOR, COMMITTEE CHAIR

While this topic has been covered quite extensively by others over the years, it will be useful in the context of this guide at least to sum up the key roles that a council and its component parts are expected to play. These more generic roles will be enhanced or diminished by the nuances of the legislation in individual provinces. (While there are some differences, the core elements tend to vary little from jurisdiction to jurisdiction.)

ROLE OF COUNCIL

In very general terms, the purpose of a council is to:

► act in such a manner as to ensure that the municipality is providing what various pieces of legislation refer to as "good government";

► ensure that the municipality delivers those services and programs that the council believes to be desired or needed by the community; and

► act in such a manner as to develop and maintain safe and viable communities.

Provincial legislation permits a council to pass by-laws and/or resolutions that enable these things to happen in a planned, fair and responsible manner. Local governments are accorded the authority to provide leadership and governance with respect to those matters within their realm, including but not necessarily limited to:

► safety and health;

► protection of property;

► planning and usage of property;

► transportation and related matters;

► delivery of services;

► setting of tax levels, issuance of tax notices, collection of revenues;

► business and business activities; and

► public utilities matters.

Councils are provided with the mandate of ensuring that policies and regulations (procedures) are put into place that enable the administration to carry out approved services and programs, and to fund them to the extent permitted by a council-approved budget and by-law. Legislation also requires that such programs and services be evaluated by council.

A council may delegate certain powers to other bodies, but must retain the authority to:

► approve by-laws;

► adopt the budget;

► approve the hiring, firing, performance reviews or changes to the contract of the chief administrative officer; and

► determine any appeals that council is required to decide.

Expressed another way, and discussed below, the principal roles of a council are to guide, guard and govern.

Guide

This role requires council to:

► develop vision, values, goals and priorities; and

► develop/evaluate policies and programs.

That is, the role of council involves setting the planned direction through identifying the vision of this council to the organization and through the establishment of those priorities that will assist in accomplishing that vision. As a complement to the visioning role, council also guides the community and administrative organization through the development/approval of policies, and through the budget review and approval of new programs.

Guard

Council is responsible to:

► ensure people and fiscal resources are protected; and

▶ ensure practices are in place to implement council decisions.

This conveys the role that a council has in ensuring that the municipality's resources are protected by way of appropriate fiscal and human resource policies and practices. Council will also need to have assurance
that its plans and policies are being discharged. This can be achieved
by way of the reports received from the CAO and the independent
report from the auditor.

While setting the new path is an essential first step, a wise council understands that it must keep its eye on the ball in order to assure itself
that the administration is working diligently at tackling the priorities it
has received from council. Otherwise, the agenda of the day will be a
continuation of what the prior council has established as its mandate.
While the new council may be in agreement with much of what its predecessors had decided, it is quite likely that there will be areas of
change and sometimes substantive differences.

To monitor performance of the administration through casual observation, attendance at meetings and community feedback, and to commu-
nicate such feedback to the CAO on an ongoing basis is a very valuable
role. Further, a council is either expected or legislated to provide regular performance feedback to its CAO. This should include a segment of
performance criteria relative to how well the CAO has helped the new
council move forward on its agenda. A council should also encourage
the CAO to be as innovative as possible within the constraints of policy, and to bring to council any suggested policy changes that would
further support desirable change.

Govern

The governance role requires council to:

▶ represent the public;

▶ consider the well-being and interests of the municipality;
and

▶ make good choices based on needed services and programs, with regard to the level of tolerated cost.

The act of governance is based on the desire of a council to assure its
residents that their needs and concerns will be properly and promptly
addressed. Council governs by way of policy choices, whether those
expressions are conveyed by resolution (policy) or by by-law. These

63

choices ought to be made based on council's view of what constitutes the "public interest."

JOB DESCRIPTION FOR MAYOR

Given that I have written rather extensively on this topic in a wide variety of articles (see *Municipal World* magazine and my previous book (*Cuff's Guide for Municipal Elected Leaders (Volume 1): a survival guide for elected officials*), I would prefer to simply refer you to those sources. However, recognizing that readers' time is limited, I will summarize this key role below, unashamedly drawing from and perhaps paraphrasing some of my previous writing. I have revised this material and expanded it where I felt necessary, based on the fact that other questions regularly surface with regard to this significant role. (It may be that I'll never get it quite right, as every time I write a report that includes reference to this topic, I find myself re-drafting at least a portion of it.)

There is little question that the mayor has a significant impact on the political landscape of a community. Based on reviews of the legislation from other provinces and how the role is actually played out in various communities across this vast country, it is obvious that, regardless of the person holding the office of mayor, there is considerable regard for the potential impact of the role. While not all of this is due to the legislation, the basis of authority for a mayor as the chief elected official is conveyed in the legislation governing municipalities in each jurisdiction.

In most communities across Canada, the office of mayor is regarded with a combination of respect and esteem. This is the people's choice as their chief elected official. While one can argue that the mayor has no more of a role than that accorded to other members of council (i.e. one vote on every issue), this is not how the residents of the community view this office. The mayor represents the will of the people and the resolutions of the council. When the mayor speaks, the citizens believe that the will of the council is being expressed. The vast majority are not interested in the nuances of whether or not this is a "weak" mayor or "strong" mayor system. In their view, and as portrayed by the local media, the strength and calibre of the mayor is defined by the personality of the individual holding the office. Cities have had mayors who were accorded considerable deference, and others who were viewed as ineffectual. The legislation is the same in both instances.

KEY ROLES FOR THE MAYOR

Leadership Functions

☑ Chair of regular meetings of council; consensus-seeker on behalf of all members

☑ Key spokesperson to community and to the municipal organization

☑ Appointment of members of council to council committees and to council-liaison positions on external agencies, boards and committees

☑ Authority to make recommendations re: peace, order, good government

Communication Functions

☑ Brief council members on all meetings and correspondence

☑ Liaison with the CAO

☑ Liaison with the public

☑ Key linkage and spokesperson to other levels of government

☑ Spokesperson for the decisions of council, both internally and externally; expresses the "will of council"

Monitoring Functions

☑ Acts as council's eyes and ears in maintaining an oversight role with regard to the conduct of municipal officers

☑ Ability to recommend the suspension of a municipal officer (if necessary)

☑ Ensure that the law is carried out

Representational Functions

☑ Acts in an *ex officio* capacity to boards and committees (if so permitted by legislation)

☑ Performs a ceremonial role on special occasions

☑ Main spokesperson to other levels of government

The mayor has considerable power, albeit largely informal, and can exercise this influence over the conduct of the business of the municipality. This does not ignore the fact that the mayor has only one vote on all matters and is, in many respects, co-equal with his or her colleagues on council. Rather, it reflects the fact that the public and media often tend to pay more attention to the mayor than to others on council. The mayor must therefore be very prudent in his or her use of this power, and should exercise it for the good of the community as a whole.

The image of the mayor as an effective leader is highly dependent on the willingness of the rest of council to follow the lead of the mayor and to work together. This does not dispute the right of individual council members to have independent views on all topics. Rather, this observation reflects the need of council to receive leadership from the chair, and to respect the right of the mayor to provide such leadership as best as he or she is able.

To be effective, the mayor will need to be able to solicit the agreement of colleagues on council to work cooperatively on a commonly chosen game-plan. It is also expected that the mayor will encourage colleagues on council to view accepted policy from a "council as one unit" perspective, rather than individually.

There is considerable inherent value to the community in the role of the mayor – provided that this role is clearly understood, and provided that the incumbent has the presence (or force) to maximize its potential. Without acting as one with dictatorial powers, the mayor can establish a significant presence in the region and with the province by identifying and leading key issues. If the mayor has a strong personal vision of the priorities facing the community, then the community will sense that there is clarity of purpose and that progress is being made.

While we describe the roles of a chief elected official in somewhat different terms in the material that follows, these roles can also be categorized into four key groupings, summarized in the table on the following page.

Leadership Functions

This role is perhaps the one that is seen most frequently by both the public and council alike. The mayor is expected to chair each meeting of council, and ensure that the business of council is handled expeditiously and effectively. This requires the mayor to be aware of meeting protocol, the concerns of council members, the personalities of council members, and the issues to be determined at that meeting. The mayor needs to be comfortable with power, and with dispensing authority with clarity and equality.

The mayor needs to be well-briefed by the CAO with regard to each and every agenda issue. The mayor should understand the basics of the issue; what is expected by the administration; the advantages of the proposed course of action; those who are most likely to be impacted; and what sort of public participation and/or reaction will be expected.

It is not the mayor's responsibility to guide the agenda process. While the mayor can request that certain items be placed on the agenda, as can the rest of council, the mayor should not be in the position of screening agenda packages and determining what can or cannot appear before council at the subsequent meeting. This is normally the obligation of the CAO, whose job it is (by virtue of the statute and procedure by-law) to ensure items that require the direction and resolution of council are placed before council in a comprehensive, yet expedient, fashion.

With regard to the appointment of council members to boards and committees, it is normally deemed to be a prerogative of the mayor to recommend the appointment of council members on an annual basis. This prerogative needs to be limited by two caveats. First, the mayor should consult with each councillor prior to any recommended appointments being placed before the full council. Secondly, council as a whole should approve these appointments by a majority vote. This can be perceived as a fairly significant issue, and sometimes an emotionally charged issue, given the desire by council members to serve on particular boards and organizations with which they personally have some degree of affinity. However, all members of council should be considered to be generalists on all issues, and thus should be eligible for appointment to all boards and committees. In this regard, it is wise for the mayor and councillors to reconsider this list of appointments each year, and ensure that some degree of rotation occurs during the course of a council term.

As a leader, the mayor is expected to be capable of "rallying the troops" around a particular issue or a particular course of direction. The direction, however, must be that established by the full council, rather than the mayor individually. Thus, in some instances, the mayor may be obliged to pull the full council forward together in a particular direction that he or she may not have supported at the outset. This obviously requires someone with the ability to lead based on decisions established by consensus, rather than someone who can only lead if the consensus reflects his or her own opinion. While this is a difficult matter, the mayor is nonetheless one individual who must be able to draw disparate views together, and enable a consensus to be reached.

Likely one of the most difficult tasks of any mayor lies in the expectation that he or she will be able to find the common ground between council members amidst the sea of diverse opinion. This task is daunting at times, due to the disparate positions that may be vigorously held by other members of council. As the leader of council, however, the mayor is expected to draw the views of council colleagues together, and to point out a reasonable compromise if one exists. The mayor needs to retain impartiality on the issue until it has been presented to council, and until it is appropriate for the mayor to voice any personal views on the issue. While the mayor is not expected to compromise personal principles, most issues have within them the potential for agreement, provided that people are prepared to see each other's point of view. The difficulty, of course, is convincing everyone that some degree of compromise is needed to reach a reasonable solution.

The vast majority of the power in the mayor's office is more implied than it is stated. The office of the mayor carries with it considerable perceived clout in the community, given the status and respect that most people accord to that office. While it may not have much additional formal power than that of any other member of council, the mayor is expected to be the leader of the community, and to be capable of taking charge of the issues. The mayor also has an implied obligation to convey the will of council to the public, whether or not the mayor has actually supported the decision of council. The public needs to know what the council has decided on a particular issue, and this is a role that the mayor is ideally suited to play.

Communication Functions

One of the keys to effective leadership is the ability of a mayor to ensure that the council as a whole is well-briefed at all times with regard to the information that the mayor becomes privy to as a result of his or her office. Council members generally understand that the mayor may become privy to information and/or concerns as a result of his or her leadership role in the community. While this affords the mayor with advance notice of such issues, or even of potential new projects, the mayor has an obligation to immediately inform his or her colleagues on council, and to inform the CAO as to the nature of those discussions. Indeed, it is preferable that the mayor strives to have either the CAO or the deputy mayor present in such discussions.

Due to the prominence of the office, the mayor may often be briefed on issues prior to the rest of council. Such a briefing will generally come via the CAO and, in some instances, by virtue of the mayor's greater degree of access to officials in other orders of government, and even the public. This additional access to information places the mayor under some obligation to ensure that the rest of council receives a full briefing of such issues, so that they are cognizant of all the relevant concerns and potential remedies. It is not wise to ever withhold information if the mayor expects the council to want to work together under his or her leadership. Thus, the mayor and the CAO will need to establish a mechanism that ensures that all members of council are equally and concurrently advised of the issues as they develop.

In part due to the position as leader of council, and in part due to the more frequent presence in the municipal office, the mayor is expected to be council's main spokesperson to the administration. This role is particularly important as a means of ensuring that the views of council as a whole are understood at the senior levels. The mayor needs to be able to advise the CAO and senior staff as to council's anticipated view of a matter, or to clarify a policy position, or explain a particular grievance as expressed by council.

Case in Point

Council went into closed session at the conclusion of a regular meeting to discuss "a personnel matter." They asked that the meeting be limited solely to members of council. While this irritated and offended the CAO, he complied with the wishes of council. One of the councillors spoke at length in the meeting regarding comments she was hearing from some of the staff that the CAO was taking longer than normal lunch breaks, and also leaving early from the office. While all of council warned against always buying into the gossip in the office, they also advised the mayor to take up the concerns generally with the CAO, but not to be specific about the source of the complaint. Several did not think the CAO had been guilty of such practices, and another felt that the extra time put in by the CAO should count for something.

The mayor expressed his view that the CAO was always there first thing in the morning, and always available for evening meetings. The mayor thought the complaint to be "petty," and berated the councillor for bringing the matter forward. In any event, he said he would brief the CAO.

Later that month, when council as a whole got together with the CAO to discuss his performance review, this matter was brought up by several councillors who felt that the problem had escalated, and that the CAO had been "thumbing his nose" at council. The CAO responded that this was the first he had become aware of the criticism ...

This example speaks to the importance of the mayor acting in concert with the wishes of council, regardless of whether or not the mayor is in complete agreement with the concerns of fellow councillors.

By the same token, the mayor needs to be careful that his or her actions do not lead the rest of the organization to conclude that the mayor has become the administrator. The mayor, like all members of council, needs to defer to the CAO on staff issues, or run the risk of severely damaging and undermining that office. This is one of the reasons why the mayor needs to be careful in how accessible he or she is to members of staff other than the CAO, unless such meetings are held with the agreement of the CAO, or at least the CAO's advance knowledge.

Monitoring Functions

The mayor has an implied obligation to monitor the delivery of local government services. This does not imply that any member of council, including the mayor, is to directly supervise the work of the administration. Rather, the mayor must maintain an awareness of what services, programs and policies are being implemented, and continually assess whether or not these are meeting community needs and standards. This can be achieved through simply being aware of what is going on in the community, and bringing any important issues to the attention of the CAO. If the matter is within existing policy, the CAO will endeavour to act upon the mayor's suggestion; if the matter is deemed by the CAO to be beyond the present council policies, then he or she is required to bring such a matter back to the whole council at a duly called meeting for council's resolution.

In this process, it is possible that a member of council may believe that a member of staff has acted inappropriately. This should not result in that council member publicly criticizing the staff member. Rather, such matter should be brought to the attention of the CAO to use his or her authority and to act as deemed appropriate, given his or her assessment of the situation.

Regardless of the rationale for such criticism, there should never be any direct public criticism of the administration by any member of council. The mayor should immediately rule such comments out of order and re- mind councillors of their commitment to this protocol. The appropriate place for negative comments vis-a-vis administrative performance is in a closed meeting between the council and the CAO.

There also needs to be a clear understanding by all parties that the appropriate protocol for a member of council in accessing administrative advice (at a council meeting) requires referral of such enquiries to the CAO for his or her response. It should be up to the CAO to determine what response is appropriate, and whether or not he or she has sufficient information to answer the question, or whether the issue should be referred to another member of the administration. It may well be that the CAO recognizes that the issue is linked to several others that are already under review, and thus the best response would be to defer any answer. Council should accord the CAO this courtesy.

Representational Functions

The mayor, by virtue of office, may be appointed to various boards and committees. These bodies are often appointed by council and may consist, at least in part, of public citizens who are asked to advise the municipality on one or more key functions (eg. planning, recreation and tourism). The presence of the mayor is often sought when a group wants to:

➤ ensure ongoing support by council;

➤ increase the likelihood of council being informed as to the issues; and

➤ obtain at least an insight into how council may react to a particular recommendation.

It needs to be made clear, however, that the mayor's role is to reflect the views of council (as they exist in terms of policy, resolutions, by-laws and informal debates/discussions) to the external agency. If the advisory agency presumes that it is hearing the word of council, only to find out that the mayor's opinion was very much a minority viewpoint, problems of credibility will result. As well, the role of the mayor as a liaison (similar to that of any member of council) rather than that of advocate must be made apparent to any and all advisory agencies.

Every mayor across Canada is expected, from time to time, to perform certain ceremonial duties. These can range from the annual parade to greeting the premier on a speaking tour. Unless otherwise committed, the mayor is expected to be present and carry the civic colours. This tends to build a real sense of community pride and accomplishment, and thus the importance of this role should not be diminished. While these events are important, not all need to be attended to by the mayor. Depending on availability, size of the event and other demands of the mayor's office, the mayor may want to delegate such an appearance to another member of council. This delegation to individual council members should be rotated regularly to avoid any appearance of favouritism.

As the official representative of the community, the mayor will frequently be in a position of hosting visiting groups and delegations. This will require the mayor to have some latitude: any expenses incurred by the mayor in hosting such organizations, delegations or individuals should be legitimately picked up by the city. An appropriate record-keeping process, as recommended by the CAO upon the input of the external auditor, should be determined. A reasonable budget needs to be established for this purpose on an annual basis.

The mayor is also expected to be the key representative of council in meetings with other municipalities (unless delegated to another member of council) and other orders of government. Any liaison on a political level should normally be conducted through the mayor's office. When another order of government is pondering new legislation or a new regional or local project, they expect to receive the opinion of council when dealing with the office of the mayor. While that role may be delegated on occasion to another member of council or a committee, it should, as a matter of protocol, be voiced and/or coordinated through the office of the mayor.

While there are often additional powers and prestige attached to the office of the mayor, these powers are only effective when supported by the rest of council. This serves as a useful check upon the authority of not only the mayor, but also council as a whole. There needs to be a genuine recognition of the value of working together and finding consensus on the issues. This will require respect for the right of each other to hold views that are at variance with others on council.

This respect should be conveyed not only at the council table, but publicly as well. That is, the public and staff of the city should not hear a council member or the mayor publicly deride one of their colleagues, regardless of the circumstance. That would be unprofessional and not serve any constructive purpose.

JOB DESCRIPTION FOR COUNCILLOR

While I have written about the role requirements of a municipal councillor (also known as an alderman in some communities) in previous reports, the number of questions that arise during such studies and at conferences across Canada leads me to believe that this is one topic on which much more could and should be written. And, although there are various requirements of an elected official according to the "municipal Acts" in each jurisdiction, none seem to be overly descriptive, and perhaps rightly so. Much of what a council member does is developed "on the fly" in response to the circumstances and local conditions. There are, however, certain other duties that are more generic across Canada. These are summarized on the following page, and discussed further below.

Represent Others

Every elected official holds their position at the discretion of the electors. No one is entitled to office, regardless of how long they have served or how successfully. They retain the support of their residents through hard work, continual focus on local issues and ongoing contact with a broad cross-section of the people who make up the community. While council members may have few mechanisms available to them to discern the will of the public, they should listen to the voices around them and seek out individual comment wherever possible.

GENERAL DUTIES OF COUNCILLOR

- ☑ Represent Others
- ☑ Govern Collegially
- ☑ Set the Direction for the Community
- ☑ Prepare for Meetings
- ☑ Build Consensus
- ☑ Represent Council Interests
- ☑ Maintain the Municipality's Best Interests

Remembering that citizens are the target audience – and not the staff (nor other members of council) – is absolutely central to successful citizen representation. This requires encouraging to the public to become involved in the political process, and efforts to ensure that there are avenues available for useful and timely input by the public. It does not require finding ways by which the public becomes involved in all issues, or even a majority of them. Rather, an elected official should be concerned with removing any apparent barriers to public participation that do not seem to be reasonable or necessary.

Govern Collegially

There are two related components to this fundamental task. One is to place the focus on governance, rather than the details of administration. The second is to seek to work together with council colleagues in arriving at decisions that best reflect the interests and needs of the population. Governance necessitates placing the focus on "what is to be done." Administration, on the other hand, has as its major focus "how to accomplish policy objectives in an efficient, effective manner." The lack of any real focus on what needs to be done unfortunately results, almost consistently, in an inordinate focus on approving the work targets and decisions of the administration. A more focused council would willingly leave these issues to an administration they trusted.

Governing collegially does not mean that a council member has to act as though he or she is in agreement with everyone on council on each issue. There is a distinct difference between being generally supportive and polite, and being viewed as part of a halleluiah chorus. It is possible to maintain an individual identity and still be viewed on many issues as "on side" with the rest of council. This sense is important to others on council because they want to feel as if they are part of a team ("we're in this together"), and not as antagonists.

Case in Point

A councillor is elected in a by-election. She makes a point of describing herself as a "disturber" and sees her role as being a "watchdog of council." The rest of council are not amused. They have served together for over three terms and enjoy their fellowship (including a few "swallies" together after every council meeting). Their new colleague makes a point of not attending these social get-togethers, and speaks ill of the practice. By the end of the first meeting of the newly constructed council, it becomes painfully evident that she is going to be the "odd one out" on most issues and, in fact, seems to take great pride in voting against even the most routine issues (eg. accepting the minutes).

Within a few meetings, the mayor and other councillors begin to ignore the questions by their new colleague on council, and reduce their already limited discussion of the issues for fear of being misrepresented in the press. She, on the other hand, forms an alliance with the community's ratepayers group. In attendance at their meetings, she is treated as their "ace in the hole." This simply infuriates the rest of council.

Set Direction for Community

This is the one feature that is often accorded the least degree of attention, and yet the one that holds the most promise for anyone hopeful of making a real impact as a member of council. Council members are charged with setting the course and allocating the necessary resources to get the job done. Unfortunately, and all too frequently, council quickly moves into a role of reviewing a draft budget (generally guided to that stage by the prior council) and discussing and deciding upon issues that have either been left over from the prior term, or that are specific to that day. While these are important challenges, their value will seem remote if council does not step back and determine where it plans to take the community, and identify the issues that it sees as the top priorities over the next few years. Being on council is not about carrying forward the status quo. If that were true, why would anyone want to change the make-up of any council. No – the real challenge is to chart a new course, and set out the markers that will assure council that substantive progress is being made.

Prepare for Meetings

Meeting preparation is an essential aspect in the life of a councillor. While it may be onerous for some, perhaps because they have never felt comfortable with reading, learning how to review reports and discern what the key governance issues are, this is not as difficult as it might first appear. Being prepared for meetings, however, is critical to the success of an elected official.

Experienced members of council will advise that while it is important to review materials, spending too much time on all of the details contained within some reports does little to help the councillor add value at the council table.

Build Consensus

While I have written earlier on the need for the mayor as the chief elected official to work at building consensus amongst members of council, the responsibility of other members of council in this regard should also be underlined. If a council is to succeed at more than simply ratifying decisions already made by its administration, there has to be a genuine commitment by at least a majority of the members to work together as a leadership body in order to provide direction and policy-based decision making to the community and to the organization. While it would be ideal if all members of a council were perceived to be working diligently at achieving consensus, the fact of the matter is that individual councillors may believe that only their own position ought to prevail; thus, they are not prepared to find areas of flexibility or compromise. Rather, such members stake out "their" ground, and then attempt to cajole, coerce or convince others of the sanctity of their position. While they may be successful from time to time, more often than not, others simply decline to be moved into more extreme positions, and move instead towards the idle ground.

Represent Council Interests

A challenge often unanticipated by those running for office is the requirement placed on elected representatives to actually represent the views of the council to the larger community and, in certain circumstances, to advisory boards and committees. Where a councillor is asked to represent the mayor at a function, there is a clear expectation that the known position of the council (i.e. its policy) will be that which is conveyed by the councillor. This duty has caused a number of problems when the council member who may be known for their outspoken views speaks to a position that is entirely contrary to that of the council. This is both inappropriate and immature but, unfortunately, a very real possibility whenever members of council see themselves as free agents, and thus fully entitled to speak their own minds and not the will of the council.

As a representative of council on an advisory ABC (agency, board or committee) where the legislation does not necessitate the councillor to act only in the best interests of that particular ABC, there is an underlying expectation that the will of council will be communicated by its representative (provided that the will of council is known prior to an issue being debated or discussed by the ABC).

Maintain the Municipality's Best Interests

Organizations, like human organisms, must take those steps that help them retain their health and vitality. In all instances, a member of council needs to be aware of what actions contribute to the municipality's well-being, and those actions that might bring it into disrespect. While very positive and useful decisions may be recommended by the CAO on most issues, there may be some recommended actions that a council simply does not believe are either warranted or currently in the best interests of the municipality.

Determining an alternate course of action is always an option, provided that what is finally approved by the council is, in the opinion of council, the appropriate choice for the community. Every decision and policy choice needs to be seen through that perspective: what do we, as the elected leaders, believe will best serve the needs of our residents, both now and in the future?

LEGISLATED REQUIREMENTS OF COUNCILLORS

Legislation spelling out the requirements for municipal councillors has tended to become more common across Canada, and tends to follow, in whole or in part, the Alberta model. That legislation calls for a councillor to:

► consider and promote the welfare and interest of the municipality as a whole and to bring to council's attention anything that would promote the welfare or interest of the municipality;

► participate generally in developing and evaluating policies and programs of the municipality;

► participate in council meetings and meetings of council committees or other bodies to which a councillor is appointed;

► obtain information about the operation or administration of the municipality from the CAO or designate;

► keep matters discussed in private at a council or council committee meeting in confidence until those matters are discussed at a meeting held in public; and

► perform any other duties or functions imposed upon councillors by the legislation.

Community as a Whole

The legislation points to the requirement that councillors make decisions based on what they consider to be central to the well-being of their municipality. That is to say, regardless of how a councillor was elected (i.e. at large or by wards), they are not elected to simply represent a particular area or segment of the population. Councillors have an obligation to consider issues from a "community as a whole" point of view. Equal weight should be accorded to the opinions and input gathered from all quarters of the municipality. Otherwise, the question could be asked, "Who speaks for the municipality as a whole?" It would be tragic if the only legitimate answer was "the mayor."

Thus, while there is often a deferral based on respect to other members of council because of their election from a particular ward, the legitimate response needs to centre on the responsibility that all members of council have to bring issues that impact the community as a whole to the attention of council colleagues.

Participation in Policies and Programs

Council members are expected to take an interest in and provide leadership to the development of new or revised policies or programs. Although the actual drafting of new policies should begin with the administration, council's role is far more engaged than we often lead members to believe. A council is expected to lead. A council is elected based on its connectedness to the people. A council should not rely on the administration to have all the ideas. The role of a council is not simply that of "responding to or solely evaluating," but one of leading.

Council needs to provide leadership to what it sees as the needs and aspirations of its residents, and determine what resources can legitimately be provided through the budget to fund those services and programs.

Chapter 12 deals with this important matter in much more detail.

Participation in Council and Committee Meetings

The requirement to participate in meetings of council or a committee of council does not mean that all members must participate equally in terms of "air time." It does, however, imply that a member of council ought to be prepared to speak to matters of concern, and to seek the opinions and wisdom of others.

Each member should also have access to the "meeting protocol" that outlines the rules of meeting. Such rules might be contained in the procedural by-law that establishes the dates, purpose and times of meeting, as well as the roles of committees. If such a document does not specify the role of individual members, then that should be made available through a committee charter or similar document that provides the needed clarification. It is essential to remember that a member of council who has been appointed to a committee (or board) by the council (unless specified otherwise by the appointment by-law) is expected to serve in a liaison role, and not as an advocate. The latter role – that of advocate – should be presumed to be that of the chair of each committee and board, and not the role of an appointed member of council.

Seeking Information from CAO

Council has an obligation to rely upon its CAO in terms of understanding the background to issues, and determining what course of action the administration feels should be taken. While a member of council may receive input and advice from a number of sources in the community relative to an issue, it would be extremely unwise not to expect the most professional and well-researched advice to come from the administration hired by and responsible to council.

Councils should expect their CAO to have developed a communication system that ensures that the best possible administrative advice is made available to council, and that such information:

➤ is well-researched and comprehensive;

➤ has been checked out thoroughly;

➤ is apolitical;

➤ has been properly "costed";

➤ is within the legal parameters available to council; and

➤ has been vetted against current policy.

Keeping Confidential Matters Confidential

There will be times that information coming to the attention of council needs to be held on a confidential basis. Much of the business of any municipality is deemed to be public. That is, there should be few restrictions placed on members of the public accessing the information on a co-equal basis to members of council. On the other hand, there will be certain issues that are confidential in nature and that, for whatever reason (as identified by the CAO or senior staff), should be designated restricted "for their eyes only." Such issues may deal with personnel matters; legal issues that warrant solicitor-client confidentiality; the sale or purchase of municipal land; or other information that either the municipal statute or the legislation governing freedom of information and protection of privacy identifies as legitimately confidential.

The key is to err on the side of being as open to the public as possible. The public expects the business of the municipality to be open and transparent.

ROLES OF COUNCIL MEMBERS AT THE COUNCIL TABLE

There are various roles that a member of council plays while discussing and debating matters at the council table. These roles are essential to an effective council. And, while some members may play a particular role continuously, others move from role to role depending on the needs of the discussion or the timing of it.

Probing/Inquiring

One of the key roles involved in any council discussion is that of probing or inquiring to find out what else lies within an issue. While each matter on an agenda should be accompanied by a thorough report signed off by the CAO, the presence of such a report is not intended by the administration to convey a sense that "we have captured all of the available information on the issues." There is a legitimate role for a member of council to ask additional questions and to probe what lies behind the rationale, or what other options were considered before they were discarded.

ROLES AROUND THE TABLE

- ☑ Probing/Inquiring
- ☑ Holding to Account
- ☑ Seeking Compromise
- ☑ Emotional Support
- ☑ Bridging Ideas
- ☑ Reluctant Observers
- ☑ Problem Solving
- ☑ Forcing a Conclusion

Often, such people (the "information seekers") can never get enough information. They read absolutely everything sent or passed along to them. They ask for more. They seek other sources of information. They try to determine who is most likely a good source of information at the municipal office. Their style does not change much throughout the term, and they become better and better at discerning reports, and at asking good follow-up questions.

Holding to Account

Councillors play a legitimate role in holding other members, boards and the administration to account for the commitments made. If the administration commits to a certain budget on a project, then they should expect solid questions as to what went off the rails when they report a significant overrun on the costs. This should not be treated as an attempt to embarrass the administration, but rather an effort to instill the message that commitments made by the staff are treated seriously by the council on behalf of the public.

Seeking Compromise

Each council should be blessed by the presence of a member who sees it as their role to find the common ground between the other members of council. Given that the others may hold very strong opinions on certain topics, the middle ground may be left to those who find this terrain a more comfortable fit. In order for that ground to be firm, however, it may be that the compromise councillor has to argue their own position as to what makes the middle a better choice for everyone.

Emotional Support

The person gifted with a spirit of compromise (see above) may also play the role of emotional support for the rest of council and/or the administration. They abhor conflict and appreciate the gifts that God has granted their colleagues. They cannot understand why seemingly sane people must become so fractious. This member consoles those who lose a tough debate, and seeks avenues to build them up for future debates.

Bridging Ideas

As an ancillary role to the compromise seeker, each council needs someone who sees the linkage between good ideas and can bring moral suasion to bear, encouraging others to accept the notion that their good idea could actually fit with the ideas of another member.

Reluctant Observers

These members approach their role very cautiously and tend to either be very cynical about everything until they determine whether their sources can be trusted, or believe virtually everything because the administration is highly regarded (and so why would the information be in doubt). They say very little at council and committee meetings, as they quietly observe the behaviour of others. What they believe, they support. What they do not, they vote against, often while saying nothing in advance of the vote. This tends to be very disturbing to the others. They are useful as a barometer of how a meeting is progressing, and whether or not everyone is being adequately engaged.

Problem Solving

Councils invariably hit an impasse on certain issues. Lines are drawn and volatility may result. Someone at the table needs to be good at seeking solutions, whether with regard to interpersonal conflict, entrenched attitudes or a tough development issue. There are also techniques being used more regularly in the business community to outline decision options, and to weigh the critical aspects. Perhaps someone in the problem-solving mode can access such tools for council to consider.

Forcing a Conclusion

At the end of the day, a conclusion is still required. This role might be filled by someone who has the knack of seeing issues and their resolution quite quickly – or who suffers from a lack of patience! Generally speaking, such individuals do not handle prolonged debate well, and cannot believe that others are so widely divergent when, in fact, the solution is so obvious!

This "I'm in charge" role reflects those who are frequently more assertive or aggressive. These folks tend to pay little attention to the niceties of process, other than to try to identify those who they may co-op into their way of thinking, and thus who will be useful at some further stage when votes are likely to be close.

However, when members are looking wistfully at the clock as it grinds along to another marathon finish, they are pleased to have someone on the team who acts as a catalyst to decision making.

JOB DESCRIPTION FOR COMMITTEE CHAIR

At some stage in the term of a member of council, he or she may be asked to take on the role of chair of a committee, board or special agency. The role of chair is an important one for several reasons:

► The chair must ensure that due process is being followed at all meetings.

► The chair must maintain an ongoing relationship with the senior staff member who has been assigned by the CAO to that committee.

► The chair needs to respect the role of the CAO as the boss of the staff member attached to a committee of council, and not undermine the relationship of employer-employee between those two staff members.

► The chair needs to be able to convey the will of the committee to all of council. This includes the need for balance, in cases where the committee does not agree amongst its own members as to the best course of action.

► The chair needs to be able to encourage public support and involvement while maintaining control of the meeting.

RESPONSIBILITIES OF COMMITTEE CHAIR

☑ Maintain an ongoing awareness of the issues within the mandate of the committee

☑ Ensure that an agenda is properly comprised for the scheduled time, and that it has been distributed to all members of the committee and to the other members of council

☑ Ensure that the rules of procedure as they apply to committees are followed

☑ Report regularly to council on the issues under review by the committee, and identify any recommendations that would require the approval of all members of council

► This requires the chair to discourage the public from using a committee forum to attack individual staff, and to rule any such behaviour out of order.

The chair of any body is normally deemed to be the spokesperson of that group. This is an important distinction to understand and speaks to my observation that a member of council should not be asked (or expected) to be the chair of any body other than one comprised solely of council members from their own or other jurisdictions. This observation has provoked any number of responses from those who have heard me address this matter at a conference. Most councillors enjoy the added prestige that chairing various bodies affords them, and thus they bristle at the notion that this is not an appropriate role. However, when members of council consider the public's expectation that they are elected to act in the best interests of the community as a whole, then the profile of a council member being identified with a group that represents a small component of the community is rightly questioned.

It is not possible for a council member to act for all when he or she is arguing the message for a particular vested interest group (regardless of how legitimate).

Chapter 9

WHAT DO COUNCIL MEMBERS EXPECT?

Some of the confusion vis-a-vis an appropriate governance model lies in the lack of awareness by administration (and perhaps council as well) as to what a member of council expects in terms of his or her role.

Council members come from diverse backgrounds. They may or may not have had prior experience as a member of a governing body in another organization. They may have had some experience in community politics through helping someone else become elected, or through serving on various boards for community agencies. They may have attended meetings of prior councils, or perhaps not.

For the most part, they share one common denominator: a love of their community and a desire to be of service. While these are absolutely critical building blocks, prospective council members may not have clearly formulated in their own minds just what they expect from their council experience. Without a foundation of prior experience, it is understandable that new members may not fully appreciate what they might encounter, or what aspects of the job are more important than others.

This is a very important consideration for anyone conducting orientations for new members of council. Whatever is placed before them in the early stages will obviously register as being of considerable importance. Thus, if the focus of the orientation and the first few meetings of council are on the role of the administration, it is entirely predictable that the interests and subsequent questioning by new members of council will follow accordingly.

Unfortunately, there are a number of municipalities where the term of office proceeds without any discussion about what each member of council sees as their objectives – both as a member of council, and for the council as a whole. As a result, the months pass by; little is said about personal objectives; and everyone presumes that the job is somehow getting done.

Misunderstanding about the personal objectives of members of council may also stem from the inadequacy of the current orientation system (if there is one at all). Information comes at new members of council so quickly that it is akin to the experience, as someone once said, of getting a drink of water from a fire hose.

There is much to learn in this process of becoming a member of council. Whether the municipality is as large as Toronto, or as small as Highlands, BC, the learning curve can be very steep and the amount of information seemingly inexhaustible. A wise administration ensures that some information is available prior to the election, some immediately thereafter, and other sources are made available as soon as necessary, or as may be needed by members of council in order to make informed choices. In no instance should critical or key information be kept back from members of council. Such a choice by the administration will do more to undermine confidence than virtually anything else.

It is interesting to observe municipalities where the majority of council members, including the mayor, are returned to office, resulting in the almost complete inattention to the needs of the new members that this provokes. There seems to be the sadly-mistaken perception that the new folks can watch those with experience and eventually, through an osmosis-like process, begin to understand the key decision-making processes (ironically, often through the example of those least able to model good governance). Even *one* new member of council means that the make-up of the full council has changed. Each term is new, and new relationships must be built. The priorities have likely changed. Everyone in any "new" term of office should readily subscribe to the notion that being in attendance at the planned orientation sessions would be for the benefit of all.

Need for Full Picture

The basis of confidence in a local government system is its openness and transparency. The administration needs to ensure that all members of council receive first-rate information on all the key issues. Such information needs to include the most likely options, as well as an assessment of those options from an administrative perspective.

Council members should be assured that the information they receive is full and complete, and yet synthesized so that it is manageable. The objective of a CAO ought to be the presentation of information to council in no more than a couple of pages, including the issue; background; governance implications; policy impacts; budget impacts; options; and recommended option.

Case in Point

In the course of a study I was asked to conduct in the lower BC mainland, I became aware of the testy dynamics, resulting from the questions of a new council being responded to cavalierly and with duplicity by some members of the senior administration. A tax increase was being recommended to the following year's budget at virtually the first meeting of the new council. When questions were rightly asked as to other alternatives to such a negative start to a new career and term, the senior staff responded that there were none. When one enterprising councillor asked if there were any funds set aside that were not targeted for any specific purpose, he was assured that there were no such funds.

The new councillor was a bit of a pit bull, and continued to press the point at the next budget meeting of council. Again, he was assured – as were all members of council – that a tax increase was the only alternative. When he asked what the purpose was for the XYZ account as itemized in the budget, red faces resulted, along with the comment, "That's an undesignated fund."

Within a fairly brief period of time, the two most senior managers were released from their roles. Why? A loss of trust resulting from incomplete and misleading information.

Advance Notice of Emerging Issues

Council members should expect to be amongst the first of those to hear about potential community issues. As information comes to the attention of the administration, the key governance implications or elements should be disseminated to members of council, so that they are not caught unawares. It is embarrassing to council members when they find out that others in the community are more aware, or seemingly more quickly briefed, on community issues than the members of council.

The policy guiding the administration should provide direction as to what type of information needs to be disseminated and to whom. This matter needs to be handled with caution, so that council members receive an adequate briefing on the key issues, but are not bogged down with all of the administrative detail that the CAO and his or her administration deal with on a daily basis.

If an issue has the potential to become a political "hot potato," then council members need to be assured that a process is in place to ensure that it is handled appropriately. All members should be advised concurrently; the same information should be disseminated; no one should have the sense that they have been left out of the loop.

By the same token, members of council need to be reminded that the CAO and the administration should not be simply feeding councillors with administrative detail (eg. employee work schedules, copies of invoices and the attachments, copies of employee personnel reviews, or job applications). If council members do not feel they can trust the CAO to handle such matters internally, and without the overhanging and stifling presence of council members, then they ought to be examining their general degree of trust in the CAO. The absurd focus on detail by some members of council is one of the surest ways to bog down a staff, and get them focused in the minute, rather than on matters that count.

Status Reports on Issues

Similar to the concept above, the administration should be expected to provide all members of council with status updates on the key issues. While it would be overly time consuming and of minimal value to try to keep everyone updated on the lesser issues, council would be well-served if it was kept informed on those issues that were either:

▶ of importance to council based on its strategic priorities; or

▶ of significant topical interest, based on the potential to be the headline story.

There is a distinction between legitimate council interest in the major issues of the day, and a fascination with everything that the administration is doing. The CAO needs to have the confidence of council that they will be kept updated on matters of significance. All too often, councils have expected an involvement in everything – negating the authority of an administration to act on matters within its domain. Such a mindset plays into the notion of a council being overly caught up with "administrivia," which leads directly to a blurring of roles. But, there are many matters of significant and legitimate interest to a council. These need to be kept on the radar, and council members should expect to receive regular updates in terms of policy issues and potential consequences.

Prompt Follow-up on Decisions

Issues decided by council need to be acted upon with considerable speed. That is, once a decision has been made, the administration's immediate task is to take those steps necessary to put them into action. As this occurs, an "information circular" could be disseminated to council, advising that action is underway (if the issue is of significance). Ensuring that council is aware that action is being taken would likely increase the confidence of council members.

Integrity

Council members expect that their senior officials, and particularly the CAO, will act with the highest level of integrity in all that they do. They recognize that there may be any number of opportunities for their management to be swayed into doing the wrong thing by unscrupulous people.

Case in Point

I recall being asked to review a municipality where the CAO had been accused of deliberately going against the expressed wishes of council. In this instance, the CAO had recommended to council that the fire hall parking lot needed to be replaced. Council, for whatever reasons, did not approve the request. The CAO, who obviously saw this as a matter of greater importance, requested a local paving contractor to add some fictitious costs onto other municipal work and, with the added profit margin, pave the fire hall lot. Somewhat surprisingly, this was done. After the next election, which occurred shortly after this incident, the mayor became aware of this and recommended to council that the CAO be fired.

When I discussed this matter with the CAO, he admitted what he had done and expressed "I'll never do that again." Suffice it to say that the council lost faith in his integrity, and decided to sever the relationship.

Public Support for Tough Decisions

The administration is not expected to go out and "sell" the decisions of council. They are simply expected to carry them out. On the other hand, there may be a number of instances where council has struggled with an issue that may have provoked division in the community. Even if the administration is not overly supportive, there still should be either tacit acceptance of the actions to be taken or muted criticism.

Common Treatment for all Members of Council

All members of council are equal. They need and expect to be treated that way. While the mayor may have more connections to the administration through more frequent contact, he or she cannot function independently. A council is a team and will only work as a reasonable, coherent and cohesive body if its members are viewed in that light. Providing exclusive information to one member of council is a sure-fire way of ensuring that council members begin to view the administration with suspicion.

Common Commitment to Public Service

Council members want to know that their administration is doing all it can to act as servants of the community and build an atmosphere of mutual support with its residents. This can only occur if both council and the administration are working diligently together in support of common objectives.

Concerns of Minority are Respected

Local governments need to work towards solutions that reflect the will of the majority, while being cognizant of the needs and aspirations of the minority. Everyone understands that the nature of local government is based on an attempt to match the will of council with that of the majority of its citizens. At the same time, it is too easy to overlook the concerns of the minority, which also should be heeded and reflected where possible in such decisions. Council and staff members alike ought to be able to discern the impact of policies on the less fortunate in society, and take steps to ameliorate the impacts where possible.

Development of Team Environment

It is the desire of most members of council to work in a wholesome team environment that reflects a clear recognition of the separate roles of council and administration, together with a sincere respect for the uniqueness of each role. This is based on a desire to treat one another with respect and tolerance. It requires the development and active maintenance of a collegial environment based on trust in one another – both between members of council, and between council and its administration. This, in turn, relies upon the development of a clear corporate sense of direction and priorities, as well as policies that guide the day-to-day matters.

Governance Model that "Works"

Each council wants to function in an environment where the role that they play adds value, and the decisions that they make are significant to the well-being of their community. Each wants to believe that their decision-making process functions as well as it could, and that if there are issues that seem to place sand into the wheels of progress, changes are quickly adopted to deal responsibly with such deficiencies. Unfortunately, of course, this is often not the case. Problems in council's style of functioning are not addressed very well, and the fundamental and underlying structural problems are allowed to persist.

In Summary

It is interesting to note that councils that function poorly cannot understand that there are others that function quite differently. Being smug in
such matters is dangerous, as the adage "pride goeth before a fall" often
comes into play.

The expectations outlined in this chapter are generic to councils. Not
all councils function equally well in each aspect described. Nor is this
range of expectations always sufficiently fed by an attentive administration. Sometimes, the ball is dropped. It may not be deliberate, but
can occur nonetheless. Most councils would afford their administration
some leeway, provided there is general recognition that the appropriate
motivation is being followed, and that staff are committed to quality
public service.

Chapter 10

IMPACT OF CAO ON GOVERNANCE

Given his or her impact on council's decision making, and impact on senior management (and staff) performance and perceived sense of integration, the CAO is a key element in the system of local government. The CAO's relationship to council, as discussed further in Chapter 11, is critical to the successful functioning of the municipal organization. It is therefore important that this relationship has, as a foundation, a solid understanding of the role of the CAO.

Policy Advice

One of the main roles of any CAO is that of acting as the council's principal policy advisor. The issues presented to council should be those that are significant to the well-being of the community. These should always be accompanied by the written advice of the CAO, and should include reference to any existing policy that may need to be changed or waived, or to a proposed new policy that ought to be drafted by the CAO and presented to council.

The CAO should take forward to council any issues that he or she is not familiar with and that are not matters subject to a current council policy or by-law. Advice on such issues should be provided to council in written form clearly outlining the key elements of the issue and including a recommendation as to the appropriate action by council. Concerns of residents should be highlighted, with advice to council as to the essence of those concerns and any action taken. The services provided by the organization must be clearly defined, and in concert with expectations of residents.

The CAO should ensure that position descriptions reflect actual and current duties provided by each of the personnel, and empower staff to take action on their areas of responsibility. It will be important to provide support for staff in the face of any criticism from the public or from the council; to take corrective action vis-a-vis poor performance where that is justified; and to provide confidential performance feedback to staff on an annual basis.

Efforts of staff should be coordinated through regular (preferably at least once bi-weekly) meetings. Ongoing and relevant training for staff is essential, and the CAO should advise council of courses available, and identify those that are applicable and appropriate to particular members of staff.

Compensation plans and personnel policies must be appropriate and fair for all employees.

Assistance to Council in Direction-Setting

As discussed later in Chapter 11, council has the principal role in setting forth the vision for and with the community. However, this does not happen in a vacuum. The CAO is expected to play a significant role in developing the approach to be taken by council in articulating its views, as well as providing advice to council on both current and future issues that need to be taken into consideration.

The CAO should provide council with background information about what has been done by prior councils; the role of planning with regard to the budget; the impact of past plans on the work of the administration; the projects that have been previously committed to by the current or a prior council; and the impact of public consultation on the community's priorities.

What the CAO should not do is provide council with a comprehensive draft plan and ask for its approval. Baptizing the will of the administration is not a good example of council's vision.

Leadership to Administration

The CAO is expected to play the predominant role in acting as the team leader of the administration. In this respect, the CAO acts as the key linkage between the policy makers on the one hand, and the policy advisors and implementers of policy on the other. The CAO represents the narrow portion of the hour glass; information and advice going to council needs to be cleared through his or her office, while the direction from council and guidance on how the will of council is to be discharged also flows downward from the CAO.

The CAO needs to have a thorough knowledge of the programs and services offered by the municipality. And, while not expected to be the expert in such matters where there are qualified staff leading those departments, the CAO still needs to be sufficiently briefed as to the key directions and issues being faced by each department and/or service area.

The CAO is also responsible for directing/choosing who is to be hired in the key senior positions in the organization. Any position reporting to the CAO should be hired by the CAO. Any position reporting directly to a department head should, with few exceptions, be reviewed and approved for hiring by the CAO. The request for new positions should be approved by the CAO, as should a recommendation to change the organizational structure.

Managerial procedures should also be the purview of the CAO. While the council is responsible for establishing the policies of the system, the CAO needs to ensure that those policies are supported by effective administrative procedures. In larger centres, the CAO will also be charged with the development and approval of administrative policies.

Relationship Building with Council as a Whole

One of the key components of a well-rounded performance review system is an assessment of the relations that the CAO has developed and maintained with all members of council, including the relationship to the mayor. (More attention is given to this subject in Chapter 11.)

It needs to be made clear that the role of the CAO is set out in legislation as being subservient to the council as a whole. This is an important distinction in that all too often the mayor or a powerful council member will exert influence over the CAO as though they had ownership of this role. Such a misapprehension of roles should never be tolerated by other members of council as it establishes a dangerous precedent for future CAO relationships, and because it is contrary to the law.

The CAO answers to council as a whole. The CAO's reports should be addressed to the "mayor and council members," and any advice presented to one should immediately be copied to all others on council. While the CAO's relationship to the mayor will reflect the greater necessary contact with the chief elected official, the CAO must ensure that the proximity of that relationship does not interfere with the separation of roles. The mayor acts as council's liaison to the CAO, and will pass both information and comments along that he or she feels are significant. That relationship, however, must not grow into something it is not intended to be.

It is useful for the CAO to draft, for council approval, certain protocols that establish how this relationship will function. Such protocols should include procedures for:

➤ giving direction to the CAO;

➤ giving direction to other members of the administration;

➤ contacting staff for information/advice;

➤ accessing preliminary research reports;

➤ using office for private meetings;

➤ the distribution/use of information by council members;

➤ accessing legal advice by the CAO;

➤ defining the role of CAO at meetings with other political leaders; and

➤ defining the role of CAO in approval of council members expense accounts.

Fiscal Management

Ensuring that the financial affairs of the municipality are being properly managed is also a requisite function of the CAO. While local governments often associate that responsibility with the treasurer or director of finance, the person most accountable for the fiscal health of the municipality is the CAO.

Such a statement is not contrary to any delegation of responsibility to the treasurer. Rather, it is a reflection of the principle of personal accountability of the senior officer. The former (the treasurer) is the person most likely to have the best grasp on the financial affairs of the community. The latter (the CAO) is the key member of the administration who should be held accountable by council for ensuring that the fiscal affairs of the municipality are always maintained in a sound, healthy state. It is therefore incumbent upon the CAO to choose someone for the important post of treasurer who has the requisite skills and academic preparation, realizing how important that role is to council and residents of the community.

CAO-Staff Relationship

I am continually reminded that the CAO has at least one other very significant audience with whom to maintain a high degree of confidence. The administration holds the keys to whether or not the decisions of the council are being translated into action. If the CAO and his or her senior staff are on the same page, then it is likely that the decisions of council will successfully work their way down the system. Where senior staff lack confidence in the CAO, that undercurrent of non-support will send waves across the organization, and will result in discontent, low morale and poor performance. The CAO must be the team leader; in order for that to happen, the CAO must be able to engender respect for his or her role. This is one of the principal challenges facing a new CAO, particularly for one who comes to the job without much (or any) public sector experience at the senior level.

As CAO, one of the primary functions is to provide both a directing and coordinating role vis-a-vis other staff. The CAO is to be responsible for the functions and activities carried out by subordinate staff. While it is apparent that the CAO will need to know something about each of their areas of responsibility, it is equally evident that the CAO will need to rely upon the expertise and academic training possessed by each of these individuals.

Relationship with Public

The CAO also has an important role in setting the tone of the municipality's relationship with the public. If the CAO sees the public as the client – and the most important audience that the staff have for their work – then the responsiveness of the CAO will underline this sense of closeness to the people being served. If, on the other hand, the CAO is seemingly more interested in the technology of city hall, and his or her outside involvements, then the administration as a whole may respond with indifference to the needs and complaints of the public.

Local municipal officials must be prepared to respond to all sorts of demands, both reasonable and unreasonable. There are times when the pressures are heavy and responses to the public may not be made in as courteous and polite a manner as they might otherwise be.

The CAO and all other staff members must remember that they serve the public, and that they are the people who represent the municipality to that public. The job is not always easy, but a positive attitude toward the public will not only help – it should be considered as essential.

Quality of Reports

The principal mandate of the senior staff, particularly the CAO, is to advise council as to its policies, programs, decisions and budget. The CAO is normally selected based on expertise and experience. Those are the qualities that council wishes to "tap." Such advice should be prepared and delivered by the CAO to council in advance of any meeting (whether committee or council).

It is ultimately the CAO's responsibility to check each report to council in light of the following:

➤ Does this issue need to be decided by council?

➤ Is this issue of considerable political interest to council?

➤ Has the appropriate format been followed?

➤ Is the information complete?

➤ Is it well-written?

➤ Do I agree with the recommendations? If yes, have I signed it off; if not, have I attached my own report?

In the final analysis, it is the responsibility of the CAO to ensure that any reports to be presented to council meet the stated (written) standards of quality and completeness. This does not require the CAO to defer or dismiss reports with which he or she may not fundamentally agree; rather, it requires that the CAO ensure that his or her own opinion, if contrary to that of the writer, is presented to council as the covering document. In some instances, the CAO might wish to request council to defer or delay a decision until the management has had further opportunity to study the issue.

Conclusion

With so many expectations placed on the CAO, the importance of choosing the right person for the task is clear. So is the need for that individual to be able to work effectively with and have the support of council. That aspect is the subject for the next chapter.

Chapter 11

WORKING WITH YOUR CAO

An effective council governance model includes a solid, healthy and respectful council-CAO relationship. Such a relationship reflects:

► trust between the council and CAO that is unwavering and based on commitments made and undertaken;

► respect for the role distinctions of both parties, and an understanding that the success of one requires fair consideration for the other;

► a willingness by council to defer administrative matters to the CAO with full confidence that such matters will be dealt with in a manner that is consistent with approved policy and legislation;

► confidence that if the CAO commits to undertake a particular action, there is no need for the council to inquire later to see if that action had been carried out;

► understanding by the CAO that there are and will be highly political matters that council will want to be seen to lead;

► a desire by council to delegate to the CAO sufficient fiscal powers to undertake significant council-approved projects without continual inspection and questioning by members of council; and

► a commitment by council to regularly review and discuss this relationship and the results of the work of the CAO, and to ensure that the CAO is being appropriately compensated for this work.

Council-CAO Relationship

If this relationship is working as it is designed to, we would expect to see council members being confident in their capacity to set the key directions of the municipality, while relying with absolute confidence on the CAO to discharge council's intentions and ensure that the administration is being guided effectively. The relationship would be marked by a deep and abiding degree of respect, and the relationship between members of council and the CAO would be marked by a collegial atmosphere and a sense of being in the business of local government as partners with very different roles.

There must be a strong base of confidence between the two distinct roles or the system will falter badly. While this takes time to build, it can also be shattered fairly quickly. Council needs to know that the individual holding the position of CAO is fair-minded; astute; of strong character; able to resist the temptation to stray over the blurred line separating policy and administration; capable of retaining confidences; willing to be a strong leader for the staff; able to work in a team environment; and of high moral standards.

A municipal system can survive many assaults or inadequacies, such as insufficient planning; too few (or too many) staff; limited policy development; interference from council in administrative responsibilities; etc. Such considerations are a part of the environment that municipal organizations face on a regular basis. But, the municipal system virtually ceases to function as intended where the relationship between council and its CAO is not reflective of trust and confidence. As the policy-making body, council has to feel confident in the advice it receives prior to making decisions. It also has to be assured that these decisions are being carried out promptly and responsively. Further, council needs to be assured that the public are being well-treated by staff, who adhere to policies and who try to reflect the attitude of council towards the public.

Review of Performance

One of the most critical elements of a successful council-CAO system is some method of ongoing, regular and formalized feedback. Such a review ensures that the relationship between council and its CAO remains positive and healthy. Further, it is essential that council continuously monitor the separation of authority between it and its CAO, and how that authority is being discharged.

While performance is being continuously monitored, there must be an agreed upon date for council to sit down with the CAO to review performance expectations and results, and to establish new objectives. Such a system should mitigate against problems in this critical relationship, and should enable any issues to be dealt with expeditiously.

RESULTS OF A STRONG COUNCIL-CAO SYSTEM

☑ Strong policy advice to council to aid in its decision making; well-researched opinions on the key issues and apolitical advice on how such issues should be handled;

☑ A sound team atmosphere for all members of staff; coordination of all staff so that the needs of the community supersede all other considerations;

☑ Discipline throughout organization; acceptable behaviour within council's approved rules; enforcement of policies as authorized by by-law or council policies;

☑ Effective use of staff resources; avoidance of any unnecessary duplication; combining job duties as necessary;

☑ Strong fiscal management systems; solid grasp of municipality's finances; ongoing advice to both council and department heads; assistance to other senior staff, so as to improve their financial management skills;

☑ Positive administrative leadership and ability to instill a good work ethic in all staff; sense of "mentoring" of solid management skills;

☑ New techniques and ideas; encouragement to come forward with better ways of doing work that needs to be done;

☑ Positive human resource management systems; well-trained and motivated staff; appropriate personnel policies; balanced, comprehensive compensation policy;

☑ Enhanced employee morale through better sense of purpose and vision;

☑ More interdependent system, with teamwork evident between departments; and

☑ Strong mandate for council that concentrates on need to set political direction; and expectation that staff will be properly guided in carrying out will of council.

How Close Is Too Close?

While performance evaluation is important, it is impossible (and unnecessary) for any council to inspect the day-to-day work of the CAO, or to question the CAO on every administrative action. The CAO needs space, and that will only come about as a result of the confidence felt and shown by council members. If council believes otherwise, the clear message is a lack of trust and confidence. A sound relationship depends upon the confidence of a council in their CAO. This, in turn, relies upon an atmosphere of ongoing communication on the issues, and assurance that the primary role of council is not being overlooked.

Inviting council members to become more involved in day-to-day activities or decisions reflects weakness and a lack of either confidence or ability in the CAO. A good CAO will have the necessary confidence and authority to make personnel decisions without council's involvement. It is not that a council should not be informed with regard to changes in senior positions. That, however, is quite different than having a hand in "how" a decision is being discharged. If council is to be effectively in control, it needs to ensure that it has set the right policy in such matters. Being further involved in the details simply sends the wrong message – i.e. one of "we don't have much confidence in your ability to handle what ought to be fairly straight forward personnel or financial decisions."

Does this principle apply to small communities as well? Of course – unless the message is "we hire only those who can carry out our decisions, not those who have the intelligence and fortitude to make decisions." While a council of a very small community may want to review the top candidates for a department head position (which is done by many, and generally without adding much if any value), this should only be done at the request of the CAO (and then without putting an expectation on the CAO that he or she ought to seek council's preference as to the best candidate).

Chapter 12

ESTABLISHING A VISION AND PRIORITIES

While much has been written about council's role in establishing the vision for the community, it is apparent that there remains a significant gap between what actually happens on the ground and the approved vision. If the approach to setting vision by council is simply viewed as a process, it will become a "checklist" item. Once done, it can thus be checked off the "to do" list. And, in many instances (unfortunately including some that I have participated in), that is precisely where the vision remains. Despite any goodwill developed by the exercise, unless there is substantive linkage between the vision setting exercise and the direction of the organization in resolving issues, this will be quickly viewed as merely a passing fad.

Every group, if it is to be more than the halleluiah chorus, needs both a vision of where-to-from-here and the leadership and resources to make it happen. The terminology, on the other hand, is not that important.

At one time, organizations were advised to set clear goals and objectives. That language appeared inadequate to some theorists, who spoke of the need for strategic planning. While that remains in vogue today, some would argue that the real role of a council is to be engaged in strategic *thinking*. Others have expanded the visioning/planning/objective and priority setting world to include business planning. At a later date, others will speak to this topic using what is perceived as modern and "today's" language. They will essentially point to the need for leaders to set the course, and those administering to help in that cause, while being primarily involved in carrying out those actions that will ensure accomplishment of the approved vision.

There are essentially two distinct aspects to council's role in establishing a future direction for the community. These are: council's strategic planning; and council's role in setting the agenda for action.

Strategic Planning

There are a series of significant components to a comprehensive approach to council's strategic planning. These include a policy on strategic planning (see example on next page); council's strategic plan (as outlined in the example on page 105 and discussed in further detail below); monthly briefings by the CAO; and an annual review mechanism.

Vision Statement – The "vision statement" might be derived or identified by the election process, or through community forums or other public participation models. Because the vision of the community may not change substantially between elections, there may well evolve a different vision if the election produces a significant change in the ideological bias or demographic make-up of the council. This one step of identifying today's vision going forward is essential in ensuring that the focus of the administration is clearly guided by the current council's vision. This is not the sole mandate of the administrative team nor that of a prior council.

Mission Statement – The "mission statement" is a broad statement that defines "what business are we in." It may simply be a compilation of excerpts from the municipal *Act,* or at least an account of the mandate of a local government in your jurisdiction. The mission or mandate has a legislative backdrop to it, as that is what establishes the local government framework for action.

Community Motto – The notion of a "community motto" is based on the possibility that the actual vision statement may be relatively lengthy or complex, whereas a community motto would be captured in very few

POLICY ON STRATEGIC PLANNING – EXAMPLE

"We, the council of XXX, believe that a central part of our role is the establishment of a strategic plan that will serve to guide our accomplishment of priorities as we understand those to be. We will review our plan on at least a quarterly basis, and conduct a major review of the plan at a minimum of every three years."

COUNCIL'S STRATEGIC PLAN
SAMPLE FRAMEWORK

☑ Vision Statement

☑ Mission Statement

☑ Community Motto

☑ Core Values/Principles

☑ Council's Goals or Key Strategic Directions (a broad brush
picture), along with key (or short-listed) priorities (5-10
identified areas for accomplishment within a set time frame
– eg. 12-18 months)

words. Such a motto could be useful in conveying the intent of the community, and how it sees itself and wants to be marketed. It's tough to do that with a series of 10 vision statements! As a word of caution, there are only so many communities that can be the "Gateway to the North" – although other than Windsor and White Rock, one could make a case for the rest! The motto should be something specific and germane to the local community, and not common to the rest of North America.

Values and Principles – Core values and principles should underlie all of what you set out to do as a council. These, in my view, should be defined by the council members with input from the administration. They should reflect council's understanding of its community. Council acts as its representatives. These may be synonymous (i.e. values/principles) or defined separately (i.e. values and principles).

Value Statements – Possible value statements might include:

We value the breadth of diversity in our community.

We value the compassionate nature of people, and the fact that many want to help each other through individual acts of kindness or through community groups.

*We value the fair application of laws that preserve
our ability to use common open space as a community. We also value residents' desire to preserve to
their own use their private space.*

Statements of Principle – Such statements might look something like
this:

*We will act in such a manner that brings credit to
our community.*

*We appreciate the differing views on our council,
and encourage everyone to express themselves
clearly and respectfully.*

*We will encourage our citizens to take part in the lo-
cal government process through public forums, delegations, community roundtables and other public
participation forums.*

Goals, Strategic Directions and Priorities – Council's goals or key
strategic directions could be identified as broad brush statements within
the framework of how council sees its mandate. Thus, the following
outline might be helpful in understanding this concept:

► environment;

► transportation;

► leisure services;

► social services;

► financial viability;

► economic growth;

► open spaces; and

► protective services.

Examples of "goals or key strategic directions" under "Environment"
might therefore be:

*With respect to the **Environment**, our goal is to:*

*Ensure that our policies and plans are established
so as to preserve or improve the existing quality of
our environment.*

*Improve the environment in our community through
the creation of more open spaces and through an active tree planting program.*

Our key priorities are:

*Review current policies and plans as they impact the
environment.*

*Create a 3-5 acre park in the urban core within 18
months.*

*Promote "green days" with each of our schools, and
provide trees and plants for open spaces; start this
program by the start of the next school year.*

*Conduct a "neighbourhood clean-up your commu-
nity" day; and start this initiative within 90 days.*

The foregoing provides a sample outline of three goals and four priorities within one of the major focus areas of any community. The goal is
broad; the key priorities are very defined and time sensitive.

WITHOUT VISION, THE PEOPLE PERISH

Without vision, any path appears acceptable. Without a clear plan,
it is impossible to measure progress. Without measurement, it is
impossible to evaluate results. Without an evaluation, no reporting
to the public is possible. Without reporting, accountability is not
served. Without accountability, credibility cannot increase.

Setting the Direction for Action

An essential requirement of a strong and effective council that is capable
of leading the organization and the community is a clear focus on what
immediate steps and actions will move the yardsticks forward. Thus, not
only does a council need to meet very early in its term of office (and annually thereafter) to identify and develop its strategic plan, the approach
taken must include an identification of the tangible planks in the foundation upon which future progress might be built. This process requires: the
policy; the strategic plan; and community endorsement.

COMMUNITY INVOLVEMENT

While the concept of enabling the community to have a role in the development of a "community strategic plan" may be generally accepted by most municipal leaders, the mechanisms for doing so are often elusive or prone to failure. In order to attribute the vision and goals to the community as a whole, a council would need to find a plethora of mechanisms to access to the mind of the public. Thus, community forums could be held; focus groups established; community groups engaged; and the results perhaps substantiated or verified by a clear and focused survey.

A council may recognize the importance of developing a statement of vision and certain broad goals. However, unless the key elements of success are identified early on in the term, limited progress on the larger issues will likely result. In such situations, council's attention tends to become focused on the bi-weekly agendas that speak to issues of immediacy, but not necessarily importance. If council members considered their campaigns, and what they heard from their citizens, as well as what their own observations told them were the roadblocks to true progress in the community, they would be far more likely to actually focus on the steps to short- and intermediate-term results.

Case in Point

In one community, it may be that the unavailability of downtown parking is driving businesses and their clientele to the suburbs or to other communities. In another, the key issue may be a lack of serviced land for residential or commercial development that, while it means higher prices for current stock, also ensures the eventual stagnancy or morbidity of the community. In still another, the lack of tourism facilities may be handicapping the community's potential to attract and keep summertime visitors.

Each community will have its challenges. Each needs leaders who see those unique challenges as opportunities.

Leadership requires one fundamental basic: someone to lead. Even the best minds in the world will make little progress towards a particular direction until someone steps up to the plate and describes where the combined efforts are expected to take the group or organization. *That* is the role and value of strategic planning.

Chapter 13

Good Governance, Good Results

Good governance does not simply happen. It requires thoughtful people who have experienced the results of an inadequate governance model and who are determined to employ changes that lead to more effective and responsive decision making. Nor is good governance a one-step process that relies on people of goodwill to step into the positions of their predecessors and agree to "play nice." Kind, well-meaning folks can still yield inadequate governance.

The process I describe links clear-headed choices within an interdependent framework. Such a framework includes much of the ground covered in the preceding chapters to this book, incorporating:

➤ a recognition that quality governance is a unique and often new concept;

➤ identification of the basic tools of government;

➤ clarity of leadership roles;

➤ a recognition of what governance is not;

➤ sound governance objectives;

➤ the elements of what makes a good councillor;

➤ the importance of orientation to good governance;

➤ job descriptions for the mayor, councillor and chair of a committee;

➤ expectations of a councillor;

➤ a clear-headed understanding and commitment to the council-CAO relationship; and

➤ the importance of a council-led and endorsed vision and priorities.

Effective governance requires processes that focus council's attention on its role – not on recreating or duplicating the roles of others. It is an outgrowth of a commitment by council to exercise its responsibility for executive policy governance as outlined on the following page.

What Does Good Governance Require?

Without wishing to appear overly simplistic in an approach to governance, it is clear that good governance cannot truly be grasped without the following elements.

Appreciation of people – This sounds quite straightforward but, in reality, it proves to be as difficult an element as any. Not all members of council truly enjoy the dialogue with others. They would much rather have rapt or fawning audiences. People will bring diverse perspectives to bear. Some will have strong opinions on select topics, and some will bring forth strong views on all matters! A member of council needs to see each citizen as someone who has a right to be heard, and the right to respect.

Desire to serve others – There are many elements of municipal life that can be very satisfying, and council members will often express their appreciation for the colleagues and friends that they make during their stint on council. They might really enjoy the involvement in so many aspects of the community that a life on council requires. Others may enjoy the number of opportunities to be in front of the media or community groups. The single most important aspiration of an elected official, however, ought to be seizing the opportunity to serve others.

Willingness to learn – For the most part, members of council are relatively bright and well-educated people. While they may not have a degree or a post-graduate degree or a diploma, they understand life. As a personal example, my father never made it past Grade 8 in England during the early part of the 1900s. Yet, he was very much a learned person. He made it his business to stay on top of current events and to ask questions whenever he did not fully understand the context of an issue. Having a mind that seeks knowledge is a precious commodity. It is also one that is essential to effective leadership.

Willingness to listen to one's colleagues – It is a difficult thing to admit, but here it is: I was not always right in my assessment of issues during my 12 years on council. Now, it may have sounded to my colleagues that I thought I was, but in retrospect, I realize that the people I served with (and had the good fortune of being served by) often had an equally valid or credible suggestion or alternate solution. A member of council is respected by colleagues when he or she expresses a willingness to actively listen to the views of others.

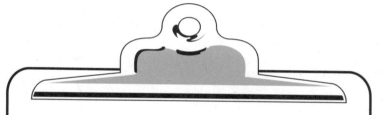

EXECUTIVE POLICY GOVERNANCE

☑ The elected council focuses on key community issues, rather than being trapped into a decision-making model that exclusively reviews administrative decisions or recommendations.

☑ Council's decision-making process embraces the notion of the right of others to be heard and respected.

☑ Council respects the right of its members to hold differing views.

☑ The mayor is viewed as an effective and fair leader, willing to share the limelight with his or her colleagues.

☑ Decisions are made in a constructive, positive environment.

☑ Policy issues are clearly identified and communicated to the public for their consideration.

☑ Major changes in direction are carefully considered, and then presented in a transparent manner to the public for input.

☑ In this environment, the opinions of staff are genuinely respected.

Readiness to compromise on issues – Most issues do not involve matters of great personal principle. Rather, they speak to matters that offer plenty of room for compromise, and the discussion of alternate approaches. Where there is a personal principle involved, stand for the principle. On other matters, seek the common ground.

Understanding of issues – It is not possible for anyone serving on a council to presume to be sufficiently up to speed on the issues without doing some homework. This requires reading the agenda package, asking questions of the administration before a council meeting, asking questions again at a council meeting, hearing the views of one's colleagues, and clearly understanding the pros and cons of the issues. Governance questions are intended to resolve such matters as: what is intended and why; what are the possible options; and what impact will this decision have on other related decisions?

Understanding of decision-making process – Good governance requires a clear understanding of the essential elements of the decision-making process. Each issue has a certain path to its conclusion. Not all follow the same path. Council members need to obtain a solid grasp of the path each decision will follow, and be aware of the points where the members will be asked either to be involved in the discussion/reflection stage, or to indicate their approval through a resolution or a by-law.

Understanding of all roles, including own – A sound definition of roles is essential to governance, wherever it is practised. This is the one fundamental issue that can confound any governance process more deeply, and add more levels of complexity, than any other. In order for there to be a healthy degree of respect, a clarity of roles must persist.

Patience – Not everyone is blessed with the patience needed to be an effective governor. For many, this attribute is weak, and yet it is critical for those who plan to stay involved in public life. While a certain degree of impatience can be useful (and even healthy from time to time, in terms of getting a process initiated or progress made towards a particular goal), those who are impatient are likely to feel very frustrated by what may often seem like glacial progress. Governments tend not to move nearly as quickly as the private sector. In the latter, an issue is identified; a solution pointed out; and a remedy applied. In the public sector, the foregoing steps may be punctuated by a multi-disciplinary review, a series of internal committees, the appointment of a public task force, and a trip or two to the provincial capital to discuss the matter with the applicable minister.

What Are the Results?

When thoughtful processes are applied by people whose intent it is to serve their fellow citizens, good things can, and often do, happen. Many of the results are unseen by most. Small changes may be made in largely procedural matters, or with respect to policies that appear only below the waterline. Many times, such changes, important though they may be, will not be identified by the media nor even necessarily reported by the municipality's own website or newsletter.

On the other hand, there will be instances when significant matters are introduced, and where the nature of the community is proposed to be altered in a substantial manner. These will be matters where all members of council need to be engaged, and where clear policy options ought to be identified. They will be matters where a healthy debate might ensue, perhaps resulting in some degree of dissonance amongst members of council. Good governance will be experienced in situations where those members involved on the "losing side" might be heard to express their view that the results were not what they wanted, but that the process was fair and above board.

The process of governance is not meant to be neat and tidy. It may become messy. But the people will be well-served when the matters are resolved because men and women of sound judgment were able to voice and vote their views – regardless of how disparate – in an open forum, and on the basis of informed comment and considered opinion.

OTHER PUBLICATIONS FROM MUNICIPAL WORLD

For further information, or to order any of the following Municipal World publications, contact us at: mwadmin@municipalworld.com, or telephone 519-633-0031 (toll free 1-888-368-6125).

By-law and Question Voting Law – Item 1288

Candidates and Electors – Item 1219

Electing Better Politicians: A Citizen's Guide (Bens) – Item 0068

Guide to Good Municipal Governance (Tindal) – Item 80

How to Campaign for Municipal Elected Office (Smither/Bolton) – Item 1284

Making a Difference: - Volume 1 - Cuff's Guide for Municipal Leaders (Cuff) – Item 0059-1

Making a Difference - Volume 2 - The Case for Effective Governance (Cuff) – Item 0059-2

Measuring Up: An Evaluation Toolkit for Local Governments (Bens) – Item 0061

Municipal Conflict of Interest Handbook (O'Connor and Rust-D'Eye) – 0050

Municipal Election Law – Item 1278

Ontario's Municipal Act - codified consolidation – Item 0010

Open Local Government (O'Connor) – Item 0030

Procurement Handbook (Chamberland) – Item 0070

Public Sector Performance Measurement: Successful Strategies and Tools (Bens) – Item 0060

Run & Win (Clarke) – Item 0020